I've Made It Through The Storm:

MY PERSONAL JOURNEY
OF HEARTACHES AND WINNING

By:

Rosemary Erickson Hunt

WORKBOOK PRESS LLC
187 E Warm Springs Rd,
Suite B285 Las Vegas NV 89119 USA

Website: https://workbookpress.com/
Hotline: 1-888-818-4856
Email: admin@workbookpress.com

Ordering Information:

Quantity sales. Special discounts are available on quantity purchases by corporations, associations, and others. For details, contact the publisher at the address above.

ISBN-13:   978-1-963718-63-8 Paperback Version
              978-1-963718-64-5 Digital Version

REV. DATE: 04/09/2024

ACKNOWLEDGEMENT

My deepest appreciation to....

All those who encouraged me and helped me in prayer, project, and financial support to bring this book to completion.

I also want to thank my family; this book would not be completed without you.

Most importantly, my gratitude to the Lord and Savior Jesus for His grace and companionship during this project and the Holy Spirit's faithful guidance through this assignment.

Author's Note

*T*hings have happened in my life that didn't need to happen. I have kept my silence long enough. I've waited until now, in my 67th year of life, to tell my truth. I can now see the end from the beginning. Age has a way of doing that for you. If you lived through the events and see it differently than I do, then just know this: I am writing MY truths from MY perspective only. You were just a bystander, watching from a distance, it wasn't happening to you. Or maybe you were the one inflicting the event on me. You didn't have to, but you did. Just as now, I am writing about MY truths, of the events of MY life, in this book.

Before I was Born

M y story starts long before I was born. My biological dad was born the seventh of seven children to Mary and Henry Erickson. My Mom was the second of eight children born to Agnes and Glen Gilder. She was a petite shy girl standing all of 5'1 and 100 pounds. Her high school and college friends told me that she was smart. In high school, she worked for the Troy Newspaper and though she majored in Home Ec. in college, I know that she also took Journalism classes for sure, and I wonder if she didn't try to minor in Journalism. She never finished college because she met my dad in her sophomore or junior year at the University of Idaho. Dad graduated in Moscow Idaho High School. In high school, he was on the boxing team. He enlisted in the Merchant Marines. Dad was just out of the Merchant Marines. Don and Carol were married at the Lutheran Church in Moscow on August 30, 1952, and had the reception at Henry & Mary's home just outside of Moscow. Don was 30 years old, and Carol was 21 years old.

I have been able to find out from high school friends, college friends and family members slowly, bits were told to me, and I was able to piece together this information with other sourced information about their lives together and it wasn't good. It was not a peaceful happy existence. They lived in Moscow for a time and then moved to Spokane, Washington. He worked for The Spokesman Review selling subscriptions and then latter, working nights for the Spokane Post Office. Mom didn't work outside the home. Dad drank, and by his own admission he was an alcoholic and stayed that way until the mid-1970's.

There is an article that I found on the internet that says that moms need a full year to recover from having a baby. This includes postpartum depression. From what I have been able to research out in medical journals and internet credible sources and by talking with people who knew her, her friends and families, she had 4 babies in 4 years. Dale was born on May 12th of 1953. Three months after he was born, Mom was pregnant again with their second baby. Unfortunately, this baby died as a result of a miscarriage. Now, miscarriages are hard to get over, as it takes time to grieve, to process through a miscarriage. You don't get over a miscarriage in three months' time. If nothing else, the body needs time to recoup, to recover and to regenerate. And then there is the mental aspect of a miscarriage. The grieving process, the dealing with the loss of a baby and the sadness.

But no, she got pregnant again very soon after the miscarriage. Randy was born on September 30, 1955, and I was born on August 29, 1956. I can well imagine that mom tried to hold it together with 3 babies 3, 1 & newborn. Living in Spokane eighty miles away from any of her family members, although mom did have siblings who came up to Spokane to help her with the children, still the responsibility fell on her. He was of no help as he was either working nights, or days and when he was home, he was usually drinking. Then came the time when the nonliving things started talking to her. The curtains and the furniture. It scared her so bad that she committed herself to a Mental Hospital in a town close by Spokane. She stayed for a short time and then came back home to her children. The boys went to visit their grandparents while mom was in the mental hospital. She was discharged from the mental hospital and a very short time later became pregnant with me. She was taking psychotropic drugs while still pregnant with me. The effects of those drugs were and still are long lasting.

Then my dad started seeing that mom would remove my plate of food from me, as she "saw that there were bugs in my food". And throw it all down the sink. There weren't any bugs in the food. That went on for a time and then my dad filled out the commitment papers to have my mom committed permanently to the mental institution.

My dad had a valent try at keeping all three of us, his kids. This is one of two pictures of my dad with the three of us, his kids. Dad is very thin looking, thinner than when they were married just 4 or 5 years previously. I always try to give my dad the benefit of the doubt and say that he tried, he really tried to take care of us 3 kids, but the stress of it all was just too much for him and he ended up putting us in foster homes. Dale and Randy were placed in Helen Dickinson's home, and I went to a foster home different from the boys. The only thing I remember about being in this foster home was that the lady would give me a bath in the kitchen sink and would always hit my head on the sink faucet.

How I Came To Live with my Mom's Parents

I n 2023, scientists and pharmacists came out with a post-partum drug that takes that depression away. Too bad that wasn't discovered decades ago. Just think of all the new mothers out there that this drug could have helped.

Mother and Dad (Agnes & Glen Gilder) would come to visit me and saw firsthand the abuse that I was getting, and they decided that it had to stop! They decided that since Randy and Dale were in a good foster home together, and I was a single child, that they would take me out of that abusive situation and bring me home to live with them. I became their ninth child. I was three years old at the time I came to live with them.

Their youngest child, Gene, is nine years older than me. All 7 of their kids took me under their wings and taught me things like how to tie my shoes, how to ride a bike, how to eat with a fork and to name a few things. They all were my aunts and uncles, but to me, they were my brothers and sisters, and still today that is how I think of them. Mother and dad didn't have a college degree but instinctively, they loved me, with a deep and wholesome kind of love. And the same can be said of these from my aunts and uncles. A deep sisterly & brotherly love. Nothing perverse about any of it. It was that love and nurturing that I grew and developed.

Mom's older sister, Phyllis, had 5 or 6 children. At this point in my writing, I do not know the details, but I do know that every one of those 5 or 6 kids were taken away from her and either fostered out or adopted out. Later in those children's lives they searched for their biological mother and found her or if she had passed away by then, they would find their other biological siblings. That is their story to tell, the reason I am telling this much is to say that, considering the alternatives, this could have very well been my story. But it wasn't and maybe that is why Mother & Dad brought me to live with them.

Though I stayed skinny from babyhood clear through my high school years, my brain had a harder time catching up. Again, after much research I discovered that my learning retention can be traced back to when my mom was pregnant with me and taking prescribed psychotropic drugs from her first stay in the mental hospital.

Another side effect of the psychotropic drugs was that ALL my baby teeth came in black and rotten and therefore all of my adult is the same, black and rotten. My folks spent thousands of dollars on my teeth. That bought me time but when I was 26 years old, I was eating Orville Redenbacher's popcorn, and my enamel teeth fell away from my silver fillings. That was when and why I went to an oral surgeon to have all the rest of my teeth pulled and false teeth became a reality.

Mother and Dad had 350 acers for farmland. Back in those days, parents never worried about if someone was going to steal or harm their children. I roamed all 350 acres, the wheat fields, the cow pastures the horse pastures and the sheep pastures. The creeks that flowed through all of them and their wet banks and the frogs that grew in them. The creek is just on the other side of the standing black calf.

My pets were all the animals on the farm, from the small bummer calves that I bottle fed along with the bummer lambs that grew up into full grown cows and steers to full grown mamma sheep with lambs of their own. Dad bought many Shetland Ponies for me to ride. Usually, they would run as fast as they could for a low hanging tree branch to knock me off them, or run as close to a barbwire fence… or better yet, run right into the barn to knock me off. I have no love for Shetlands to this day.

There were 2 gates from the county road and garage that was a lift latch and a rock walkway to the second bridge, that had a wagon wheel in a metal frame that swung open and close. On the other side of that gate, was a wooden bridge that was built over a creek and a slightly damned up water to create a waterfall under the bridge. From the bridge, there were a very huge flat rock and then stones from The St. Joe River, Marble Creek, Idaho. These rocks were cemented into three steps up and then more Marble Creek rocks walkway to the house. It was a fun and beautiful to walk down these different gates and walkways.

Just to the right side of the second gate (the swinging wheel gate), is where Goldie, dad's tall Belgium workhorse (that I loved so much and I like to think that she loved me), she would stand under the cool of a Cedar tree and would tolerate my playing around her hoofs and legs and let me ride her with no saddle or bridle. She would let me lead her to a tree stump, hop up on to her & ride her around the cow and horse pastures.

One time, I must have been about 5 or 6, I was playing ring around the Rosie's around her legs and hooves. Finally, she got tired of this pesky little girl, and she raised one of her hooves and just waited until my little foot was right under her hoof, then she lowered that hoof over so slowly and carefully, right down on top of my little tennis shoes foot. Down firmly enough to hold me there but not hurting me. Then she turned her head around and looked me in the eyes as if to say, "NOW SCAT!" and lifted her hoof and I ran away! All these years later I can still remember the tenderness of that moment.

There were coyotes that were killing Dad's sheep and lambs, so Dad had a professional trapper come and set traps. One of my chores was to bareback ride Goldie up into the sheep pasture and ride the fence line, which was where the traplines were placed, to check if any coyotes were caught. I was so afraid that the coyotes would jump up and get me. Dad assured me that Goldie knew what to do and would protect me. Besides, she is so tall that no coyotes could possibly jump up that high. I said, ok, Goldie will protect me and off we would go. There were never any coyotes caught in the traps and I rode home, safe.

We had a collie named Bluey (he had blue eyes) and an Australian shepherd with a blue eye and a brown eye, named Toby and a black Cocker Spaniel named Puppy, who loved my Uncle Richard. I loved them all so much and they must have loved me for they all went everywhere I went. Ohh! the adventures we had and imagination that I had!

I was still very young, not in school yet, Mother and I would make me a peanut butter and jam (my favorite was and still is apricot & pineapple homemade jam) and a pint jar of Nestle` Quick Chocolate milk. With the lid on it, I used to shake it up so that it was all foamy and ohh! so good! And then I would take my picnic on a hike with me. Usually, I ended up at the newly made hay wagon that Dad and Ray U made, and I would pretend to be in a storm on that hay wagon while having my picnic. Mostly, I would pretend that the wagon was a pirate ship, and a stick was my sword... unguarded mate! Usually, I ate the sandwiches as I was walking to the hay wagon, sharing it with all the dogs as we walked. The chocolate milk I saved for the wagon, and it was all mine to drink and the dogs would have to go without any.

I remember that I loved to play in the horse pasture where there was a creek with deep banks. I would lay on my stomach on the highest part of the bank and catch baby frogs and watch their crawdad being brave enough to catch some of them. I loved playing in the mud and water. There was an old supply of hauling wooden wagon that I would play Wagon's Ho! And be the master of the wagon. Dad had an old hay cutting sickle machine that I would sit up on the tractor seat and shift the gears and "drive" the machine. The picture of me with my pet calf was taken at the location where most of these adventures took place.

One time, the county road crew were replacing a culvert down by the sheep pasture on one side of the road and the horse pasture on the other side of the road. I begged Mother to let me go and watch them digging the old culvert out and replace it with a new one. Mother finally said yes, but that I had to stay in the horse pasture and not go on to the road and get in their way. I did what I was told. There was a misty rain and Mother made me wear a red scarf. I pretended that I was little red riding hood while I watched the men work. There was a car that was stopped on the road while the crew worked on the culvert. The man & woman in that car were headed to town and they got such a kick out of watching me that they decided that I was a fairy. On their way back home from town, they stopped at the house and quietly left a coloring book and some crayons and children's watercolor paints and a bottle of bubbles and a wand to blow bubbles with. They were so taken with me that they gave me a large Mother Goose Nursery Rhymes book that I still have to this day. They talked to Mother and Dad about me and asked if they could adopt me. Mother and Dad very politely said no, that they loved me, and they didn't want to give me up. The couple moved to Hawaii soon after that but sent me a letter with a seashell necklace. It's funny how kindness from strangers can have lasting memories.

Mother loved cats and I loved baby kittens. Every summer, Mother would clean out the ashes in the fireplace (in the living room) and I got to scrap the ashes into a little square hole at the entrance of the fireplace. Then I needed to go down into the dark and scary basement to see if the ash bucket was filled. If it was, I would tell Mother. Now that basement was mostly dirt with mud that came from the cistern (water tank), that overflowed. There were frogs and toads down there and even though I loved to catch those critters out by the creek… they scared the daylights out of me down in that dark basement. So to help make me brave, I would take a kitten down there with me. Then I was brave, because I was protecting the kitten. Then I would carry the kitten up the stairs and into the living room and scrape ashes some more. When I wasn't paying attention to the kitten, it crawled over to the ash hole and fell. Down, down, down into the ash bucket. I cried to Mother, "Ohh, I've killed the kitten, I've killed the baby!" Mother and I would go down and see how the baby faired. Mother would pick up the baby tenderly and brush off the ash and the kitten would start crying for its mamma. "There, there Rosemary, the kitten is fine, but you must be more careful if you're going to have the kitten up in the fireplace helping you." I was remorseful. Till the next time.

On the back porch, (the very porch that I had to walk through to get to the stairs to the basement), Mother and Dad had a large chest freezer, and on the top of the freezer, Mother would put a box filled with old blankets or cloth of some sort. This box was the sleeping box for all of Mother's house cats, kittens and yes even the barn cats would come to sleep. I loved to wake all the cats up from their naps or sleep and then watch as the cats would all stretch and stand up and step out of the box. It was like watching clowns getting out of a VW Bug. The box was big enough for three cats. Twenty cats would emerge from the box. To this day, I love cats.

When my brother Dale was 9 years old, he and my other brother Randy were crossing a street in Spokane, WA. At a crosswalk, coming home from school, when a car came and hit my brother Dale, in a hit and run accident. They took him to the hospital and removed his spleen. But did they do all that was necessary for him? They probably did for the very early 60's but they didn't do much for him. The hospital sent him back to Helen's home and there he lay for a month, maybe two. I can well imagine that this 9-year-old little boy laying there crying for his mamma. All he wanted was his mommy. Randy tells me that he was never the same after that accident. He used to watch over and look out for Randy and after he was hit, he turned mean. This makes me wonder if he didn't sustain a concussion and possible brain damage? I don't know but considering today's world knowledge of football concussions and personality changes, it does make me wonder if everyone involved did all that they could do for this child. I would have like to have really gotten to know Dale, but that was not possible, for he died just a few short weeks later. I cry for the child who just wanted his mommy when he needed her the most. He died alone and with no real family except for Randy being there with him. Someone told Mother about him dying and when she told me she took me down to the wooden bridge, there she told me that my brother had died and then she cried. I cried because she was crying. I didn't know Dale enough to cry for him, but it made Mother cry and because she cried that made me cry. I know that there was a funeral, but I can't remember it. I must have been around 6 years old at the time.

School

My birthday is August 29 and I started first grade on my birthday. I remember opening presents before the school bus came, and there were some ribbons for my hair. Mother put them in my hair and off to school I went. I loved the 1950's song, Scarlet Ribbons.

"I peeked in to say good night, and then I heard my child in prayer,

And for me some scarlet ribbons, scarlet ribbons for my hair,

All the stores were closed and shuttered, All the streets were dark and bare, In our town no scarlet ribbons, not one ribbon for her hair,

Through the night my heart was aching, just before the dawn was breaking, I peaked in and on her bed, in gay profusion lying there,

Lovely ribbons, scarlet ribbons, scarlet ribbons for her hair, If I live to be two hundred, I will never know from where, Came those lovely scarlet ribbons, scarlet ribbons for her hair."

I would sing with the record this song over and over. So, Dad made sure that I had ribbons for my birthday. (I wore them to my first day of school, first grade). I would sing at the top of my lungs and finally Mother couldn't take it anymore and told me to sing softer, and that I was tone deaf. What do you mean? "Well… you sing off key." "Oh." And guess what? I am still tone deaf today. But, in the car, driving by myself, I sing.

Back in the day, we had a TV but mostly I listened to recorders on the record player that was a stereo in a wooden piece of furniture. They used to make colored vinyl for children's stories and songs. Another song that I would play over and over again was Doris Day's, "How Much is that Doggie in the Window?"

School was the most difficult for me. The powers that be decided to hold me back in first grade for another year and that maybe I would be able to catch up with the other students. I just couldn't grasp any of the concepts. I would think, "Teacher, please don't call on me because I just don't know the answer. The term ADHD wasn't a concept until I was well out of high school. The teachers didn't know what was wrong with me, just that I was a very slow learner. "She must be mentally retarded."

That was the term used back in those days. And they treated me as such. I hated school. Hate was a mild word for how I felt.

And then there was recess. My girl classmates were kind to me and included me in all the games. The "Little Building" (first through forth grades), playground equipment were a tall, really tall swig set with changes for hand grips and was such great fun to pump higher and higher and then twist the swing and swirl around and around, till we were almost sick.

There was a slide that was almost as tall at the swings, a teeter totter, a merry go round that you ran pushing it and then when it was going fast enough you jumped onto the bench seat and road around in circles. We also had "the giant strides" that you hook one arm pit or held on to it with two hands and ran around in a circle till you were lifted off the ground. The boys loved to come and watch and see our underwear. So, we girls got our mothers to buy us some "petty pants" that looked like what Little Bo Peep wore in the Mother Goose illustrations. I remember Mother and I looked in the Sears Catalog and she ordered several pairs for me. We also had a Tether ball area and then around the corner, the area that led to the basement. This was the area where we girls played house. We swept that entrance hard and spotless, after all that is how houses should be kept! Right? Our teacher would read to us the story of "The Boxcar Children". At recess, we girls would pretend that we were the "Boxcar Children" and sweep the dirty floor of the entrance to the basement of the schoolhouse and look for broken tableware.

Out in front of The Little Building were the monkey bars. We all seemed to survive those monkey bars, giant strides and high swings and a tall slide. The steps that led from the yard up and into the schoolhouse were long and wide steps. We, kids loved to play Red Light Green Light, Mother May I and hopscotch up and down those stairs. They were safe for games that we loved to play. I remember that Dad bought me a pair of black velvet shoes. Just like the ones that Jennifer K had. I wore them out within weeks because of me dragging my feet to get the giant strides to stop. Dad was mad at me. He said he would never buy me special shoes again, but he did. He bought me a pair of black and white saddle shoes. There! Try and wear these out!

The hard part about recess was that the older girls would tease me about my mom, or that I must be related to Rosemary Clooney, "because she was as looney as a bin and so are you". "And ohh that's right, you don't have a real mom". Or "How come you don't live with your real mom and dad?" And on and on it went. Until today I can still remember who these bullies were. I also remember those people who were kind to me.

The school plays for me as a shy girl were scary but the teachers understood, and I got to be a flower or a tree. That made me very happy. The best school days were Scholastic Book Day when a big box of books would come into the classroom, we kids got to open the box and then from the order list our names were called out and we received our books. For those who couldn't order books, our teacher would order a book for each of us so that we wouldn't be left out. I usually have been able to order books.

I loved my first and third grade teachers. To this day, I will never forget them for "Kindness "as their first names for me.

Learning to Read

When I was in the fifth grade, I was the only kid on Spring Valley/ Nora Creek Road, so the school district decided that they were not going to send a school bus up that road to get me. Dad had been on the Potlatch school board and knew that was not legal for a school district to do. So he said, "Ok, we just won't send Rosemary to school this year." No fuss, no drama, just the facts.

Anna Marie Oslund was at that school board meeting and she said, (in only a voice, that if you knew her, you well remember) "OHHHH, No,No,No!! She MUST go to school! I will stop and pick her up and bring her home every day. So, she did, every morning after I would get into her car, she would start singing…. "Onward Christian Soldiers Marching off to war…." If she did nothing else, she was going to get some religion into this heathen girl.

Anna Marie was an old, retired school teacher. Later in my life, I discovered that she taught my own mom. Mom and her siblings would walk up the county road a mile to Anna Marie's School house for their elementary school years. But now, she was the high school librarian, so she had to be at the library before and after normal school hours. Years later, I read in her memoirs that I did put a crimp in her life, as she would have had dinner dates with her grandchildren but because she had to take me home to my house, she would decline the dinners. I felt bad when I read that, but still so very grateful for what she did for me.

To keep me busy while she prepared for the day, she gave me a Nancy Drew book and said "read this and give me a book report on it". As the few days went on, it was determined that I couldn't read. She sat down with me every day after that, starting with the first sentence, then I would read, then she would read. Then the first paragraph, then I would read the next paragraph. Then the page, and I would read the next page until I was reading all on my own. Again, in her memoirs she said that when she saw that a student was falling behind in reading, she would take them under her wings and teach them how to read so that they wouldn't drop out of school. This might have been me and for her taking that time to sit with me and help me to read, I owe her forever.

Years later, I was having to read through a lawyer brief and understand what I was reading and thanked God for Anna Marie for getting me started in reading Nancy Drew books. Many years later, because of Anna Marie, I was able to write a book and published it. All of these is because she took time and didn't let me fail.

When I was in the 6th grade, my brother Randy came down from Spokane to live with Kathy, our mom's younger sister. The next year, maybe two years, Randy came to live with Mother, Dad and me until he graduated from high school and enlisted in the army. Randy and I were never close, mostly my fault. I was a little snot to him all the way through his high school years. I wish I could go back in time and change things. It was during my junior high years that Mother wanted to start going back to church and wanted me to go with her. I did. It was the years of the miniskirts, and I wore my shortest one, and if anyone said anything, that was it! I was never going back. No one said anything. So, I kept going back. There were a lot of kids there that I knew from school. Soon they asked me to join the Pathfinders club and I did. I also kept going to church and was baptized when I was 16.

On the school bus, Curt Thomas used to try to beat me up but instead of that, he just yelled and scared me. I hated riding the school bus. But I guess Curt and I were more the same than we thought… both of us were from broken homes. Years later in high school we became friends and still are to this day.

In high school, I ran around with 5 different groups of kids, all accepting me for who I am. Lee Ann, Sandi and I started first grade together and still to this day we are all good friends.

For the most part, I remember nothing but good things happening for me. My first boyfriend was from Deary. My first date with him was at the Rathaus Pizza. Best pizza ever made but messy. I was scared and broke the ice at messy pizza. We laughed, talked and had a good ol' time. He taught me how to play the pinball machines and I went to my first prom with him, the Deary Jr.- Sr. high school. My first prom dress was floor length with a green ribbon around the waist. I heard years later that he is gay. I turned my first boyfriend gay. I smile because I know that is not true, but I always wondered why he wouldn't try to kiss me. He was so painfully shy about things like that.

The Car Wreck in The Salmon River

During winter when I was 16, the youth group called "The Pathfinders" that I joined had swimming lessons in the University of Idaho swimming pools. I did pretty well, but the stroke that I mastered was the butterfly stroke. That same spring, Sandi (my lifelong friend) wanted me to go with her to Nampa Idaho, to attend Northwest Nazarene Colleges freshman orientation.

We hit the road down to the college with the Troy Nazarene pastor and his wife and two baby daughters. Along the way, his driver's back tire had a flat but his spare tire had a bubble on it. With no gas station or garage close by to fix the tire, he was forced to put the bubbled spare on the car. Thinking that he could make it with no problem as long as he drove slowly. However, we were running late, and he was impatient and soon he was driving fast. Fast along a stretch of highway that runs right along the Salmon River. Just before Riggins, Idaho, there is a bridge that happens to be the location of the time zone change. About a mile from the time zone bridge, the bubble on the tire burst and threw us into over exaggerated steering motions.

At first, he was going to take the rock wall then at the last second, he chose the river. On the first flip of the car into the water, his wife was thrown out of the car and broke her neck and killed her instantly. On the second flip Sandi, in the back seat, on the passenger side and the driver, the pastor was both thrown out of the car & into the water. And I went with the car and babies into the cold, icy March waters of The Salmon River. I was knocked unconscious and down to the river floor, the car and I went. I truly believe that my Guardian Angel woke me up. And after finding an opening, I pushed myself through a popped-out window. I didn't think about the babies. I swam up to the top of the center of the river, and Sandi called me on, "Come on! You can do it! You can swim over to me". Over and over, she called me until I was on the rocks where she was. I swam the butterfly stroke because it was all that I could automatically do in the freezing waters. I almost overshot where she was, but I made it to her. We rested and then we scamped up the rocky embankment of the river to the highway and to flag down help.

We were taken by car into the town of Riggins where we were checked out at a medical clinic and the pastor called his insurance guy in Troy and not too long the whole town of Troy knew about the wreck. Sandi and I were taken to the home of two old maid sisters (reminded me of the Baldwin sisters of the show, "The Waltons"). This is where we waited until Someone from Troy was able to come and take us back home to Troy.

Conquering The Fear

I had a very real fear of the river water, any river. Until one year, when my daughter Kristal was 8 or 9, Doctor Drury asked if I wanted to go with my son on a river trip. He couldn't go as he was hauling hay, so I asked if Kristal could go and Doc said yes.

Doc was the town of Troy's doctor and in the summertime he and his wife Elaine and their 5 children had a professional River Rafting business. He trained his children well and then he also hired other very capable teens and college age boys to be the "boatmen". There is an etiquette on the river that you do, and you don't do. Doc instilled in all the crew and all the customers the do's and don'ts of the river.

When Kristal and I joined the group of rafters in the morning of the 4-day run, Doc said to me, "You and Kristal will be riding with me". Period. Docs was a "slow boat to China" and he was going to make sure that I didn't fall out. When we stopped for the noon meal, I asked if we could ride in a faster boat…. he had to think about that for a long while, but finally he consented. And that was the beginning of my love for whitewater rafting. We rafted with Doc and another professional rafter for about 3 to 4 more times before I left the church.

To The Next Generation

T his is getting ahead of my story, but also it coincides with the above life story. After I left the church, Kristal and my youngest daughter Karen still wanted to whitewater raft, so I reached out to the professional Rafter guide, Salmon River Experience, and the 3 of us would raft with them, every 2 years for about 4 different trips. Then we all got busy with our different work lives, and we just stopped going.

Kristal, however, never lost that love of the adrenaline rush of the whitewater, and so she took beginner classes in Kayaking in whitewater. I told her rafting is one thing but Whitewater kayaking. Are you trying to kill yourself? She thought long and hard about my comment and said, "Mom, I work at a very mind using, stressful job and never use any of my body muscles in this job. Kayaking is an adrenaline rush, but mom, also I am using muscles that haven't been used in such a long time. And I am quite good at this". Okay. Just don't tell me you're doing these classes and runs until you get off the river because you know I will be worrying about you the whole time. I can't help it, it's the mom in me. I love you and don't want your head bashed in (she does wear helmet and life jacket) or you to be drowned". She softly laughed and said, okay mom, will do.

Kristal was very observant to what Doc and the other professional rafting companies taught us and on these kayaking classes, Kristal just automatically does what is needed to be done without being told. Example, as she calls it, "sleeping" the kayaks up out of the river and up to the shore or trailer that carries the kayaks. It doesn't matter if it is her kayak or another person's kayak, they all need to be taken up to where they belong. She just does it. She wasn't trying to but she impressed her instructors greatly by just getting in and getting the task done. Picking up trash around the camp sites is a must. Each rafting company needs to leave the spot pristine as it was or better than when they came. She also was very observant to looking at the flow of the river, and how to "run the river" as in where to head her kayak so that if she misses the boulders in the river, she doesn't flip her kayak. A trait that she learned from Doc and another trait that her today's instructors are very impressed with Doc was the best. And I thank him for those river trips when she was so very young. His love of the river was instilled in her and me as well as Karen.

Meeting my Husband

That summer of my 16th year, I met a guy from church while a group of us Pathfinders were on a 10 or 15 mile hike up Moscow Mountain and then back down. Somehow during that hike he slowed down his walking and soon was walking with me. That was the beginning of our dating years. He was going into his sophomore year in college, and I was going into my sophomore year of high school. He was 21 and I was 16. Back then the age difference didn't seem to bother anyone. Today, however, that age difference would have raised red flags all over the place. But since we were, (in my words), "good little Advent kids" no one thought anything of it. This was the early 70's after all. Him controlling me didn't start until I wanted to attend my junior- senior banquet and dance. Oh no, you can't go to the dance, dancing is sinful. But he would make it up to me by taking me to the finest restaurant in Pullman. Then afterwards, he cried on my shoulder all the rest of the night because his grandma had just died.   The same thing happened when I wanted to attend my senior -junior dance. He took me back to that fancy restaurant and then had an over dramatic reason for keeping me from attending the dance. And again, the same thing happened when I wanted to attend my graduation night kegger. I didn't drink alcohol at all but wanted to socialize with my classmates all of whom I liked and just wanted to have one last fun time with them. Ohh no, you can't go, and again, some over dramatic reason why I couldn't go. Sandi saw through his bull... but I couldn't. I didn't understand because I was raised to think and do whatever I wanted to. I didn't know there was such a thing as manipulation.

On my birthday, my senior year, he asked me to marry him. Roses and an engagement watch and a speech that said, life as a farmer's wife won't be easy, there will be mostly hard work. I should have really listened to the words he was saying but I had stars in my eyes, I was in love, what could possibly go wrong? We set the date for the wedding to be two weeks after I graduated in high school. That whole senior was a blur of school, dating and wedding plans. All I could see before me was the wedding. I was blissfully happy and that would continue after the wedding, right? Wrong.

Wedding and Married Life

B efore we got married, his dad and him went without me and picked out and bought a double wide   trailer for them to put on an end piece of land, next to the Troy- Deary Gun Club and the family owned rock pit. The driveway was at a 45-degrees angle to the county road and up a steep hill. I had no choice or say in all this decision making, of my life, my living arrangements.

Our honeymoon consisted of going to Manito Park in Spokane. That was it, as he needed to be back home 3 days later to start cutting hay for the haying season of the farming.

The wedding was a large-scale event with 200 people in attendance. Of those 200 people, one family came where all the children had the mumps. Just two weeks later when the double-wide was being delivered to the spot where he and his dad chose, I came down with the mumps. We were staying with his folks in a camp trailer... and I was to stay in the trailer while he went back to his old bedroom. I wasn't even allowed to come and watch my house being pulled up that steep hill. But I did go, being allowed to or not-be damned. Then two weeks later he came down with the mumps too. And he stayed in his bedroom and I in the camp trailer. Finally, he got better and we-as in the three of us, his dad, him, and me set about leveling the house on the cement pads and leaving the axles on because this was a "temporary home" that lasted all my 25 years with him. He promised me that we would either build a stick home or buy a small farm of our own. Neither of which happened. Oh, he was full of promises, but he had no intention of fulfilling either of those promises.

We lived about 3 miles from his folk's home and another 3 miles farther up the highway/country road from my mother and dad's home. I was "allowed" to go to his folks once a day if I wanted to but to go to mother and dad's, well that was using too much gas. It means isolation for me.

I worked on the landscaping of the yard and the garden areas. Putting the interior decorations together. With no water in the house as the well was in the process of being drilled and then the pipes laid from the well to the pump house to the main house, I was to go to his folks for showering and laundry, but going to my folks raised anger in him. I remember we used to play chase in our own house or hide and seek. I remember that I hid in the coat closet, and he came and leaned on the door so that I couldn't get out. I went crazy with panic attack. Finally, after a long time he let me out. Then he got to throwing all the bed covers over my head and laying on top of me, again the panic attacks. Over and over locking me in rooms I couldn't get out of or laying his full heavy weight on me have taken its toll on me to the point where even today I can't go into an MRI machine without being totally sedated before going in the tube.

I had nothing to do with my time while he was at work. He went to work about 7 or 8 am and didn't get home until dark thirty, 8 or 9 pm. I wasn't allowed to work, "because my mom doesn't work, then my wife doesn't work either". I wasn't allowed to have a T.V. but we did have his expensive stereo and radio to listen to. When he was gone, I listened to my music but when he came home, it was to be religious music or nothing. I wasn't allowed to read novels, as that was the devil's work, but I could read the Bible, or religious books or biography or autobiography. Because of no T.V. in the house I went to the library every two weeks and brought home a stack of books (approved by him), this makes my comprehending skills developed with each book I read. Little did he know, but he helped me be able to write my first book and now this second book.

We didn't eat meat because it wasn't allowed by the church. I really didn't know how to cook, but with church sanctioned cookbooks and ladies of the church teaching me how, I became a decent cook. So much so, I even started having guests over after church. I did insist on eating beef, as I was not totally convinced that being a total vegetarian is the best route for the human body. To each person their own, but I am still not convinced.

I had much time on my hands, so one day I asked his grandma if she would teach me how to crochet. She was happy to teach me, in fact, his mom and dad were happy too. He was helping his dad farm his mother's parents farm in Farmington, WA. So, every few days I would ride with them to his grandma's house, and she would teach me a new stitch. This came in handy as every winter I would crochet 2 or 3 Afghan while he would tell me minute by minute details of his day.

The late 1970's -Children and Married Life

I wanted to wait for a couple of years before I started having children. We were married in 1975 and by the time 1977 rolled around, I was ready to have a child. Thinking that if I had a baby my life would get better. Jason was born in November of that year. Thinking life would get better was such a bad idea. Jason was such a cute little baby, but since I had no experience with things like colic or anything associated with babies. My constant companion were two books, the first one, what to expect in your baby's first years and the second book was Dr. Spock. I relied heavily on the first book and took Dr. Spock's book with a grain of salt.

This next part is for Jason, I am so very sorry for all the mistakes that I made with you. I wish, oh how I wish, I could take them all back. You were such a happy baby, that is until you were diaper trained and went with your dad to spend all day and night on the tractors and combines. I am so sorry I didn't stand up for you. One day, Jason was sick and in the back seat. I stopped at mother's house to get something, and we started talking, and talked and talked. Jason, who just wanted to go home, started kicking the back of the driver's seat and throwing a tantrum. I heard him kicking the seat and I came from the shop, taking his belt off as he was walking from the shop, to spank Jason. I saw him and stopped talking with my mother-in-law who stepped in front of me and said... "DON'T you DARE! This is my fault, because I stayed longer than I intended, and Jason is sick and just wants to go home, and if you do, I'm taking Jason and I'm leaving you"! And with that I got in my car and drove home. He followed me in his pickup home; I was in the house packing my suitcases to leave. He got out of his pickup and took the serpentine belt off my car engine. I went out to the woodshed and got the sledgehammer and said, "If you don't put that belt back on my car engine, I'm going to take this sledge and bust the radiator of your pickup." He did, and I didn't. But he said, if you ever leave me, I will make you walk with suitcases and children in tow. He kept threatening me that all the rest of my married life with him.

I missed having a T.V. and would go over to mother and dad's so that Jason could watch Sesame Street. One day, Mother and dad bought a new console T.V and gave me their old one. All was great until he came home for the night. He said to me, you put that T.V. out in the woodshed. And it stays there. I did carry it out. And then when he left for the days and nights, I carried the T.V. back in the house, Hiding it in Jason's closet. Later in the girl's closet. The only stations we could get were the P.B.S. stations and one very local station. One day he came home and demanded that I take that T.V. back out to the woodshed. I said "NO!" and he said that if I didn't, he would break it. I said if you do… I will not only smash your radiator but your whole pickup engine. He backed down and left the T.V. alone. We still kept the T.V. in their closet and turned it off when he came home, but he didn't usually come home until it was the kid's bedtime anyhow, so no big deal.

When we were first married, he would give me a monthly allowance for groceries and household needs. Always it was a perfect amount. Then as time went on, he stopped the monthly allowances and asked me how much I needed for groceries. I tallied it up and said $40 will do. He gave me $20. And said make it stretch, but I need MY lunch makings out of this. I would say that the majority of our fights were of money and of me overdrawing the checking account.

He wanted to stop me from drinking Pepsi, so he knocked the dollar amount down so I couldn't buy the Pepsi. The one and only vice I had was drinking Pepsi. I didn't smoke, or drink alcohol or do drugs, I just drank Pepsi, because our water was full of rust and calcium and tasted awful and turned my blonde hair rust red and all our white clothes to rust color.

I wasn't about to quit drinking Pepsi. Turns out, many years later, I found out that the caffeine in the Pepsi helped with my ADHD, same with coffee, by working on the synapses in the brain, what make over stimulations in most people, mellows and slows down the ADHD brain, and allows the person to think and physically get things done.

Mount St. Helen's Volcano

May 18,1980 was the day that the Mount St. Helen volcano blew a hole in the side of the mountain. People still talk about it until today. "Where were you when Mount St. Helen's blew?", I remember it well. I had taken Dad and Jason who was three & a half years old at the time, to The Renaissance Fair at East City Park in Moscow. There is nothing particularly interesting about that trip except that it was a day that dad, Jason and I did together, seeing all the booths and sights and sounds and eating some of the foods that were there. Then, along about early afternoon, the sky turned black like it was twilight, but it wasn't. The rumors started floating from person to person that Mount St Helen's blew and that a huge cloud of ash was headed our way. We tried our best to go home before the ash ruined the car motor. I remember thinking that the light dusting of ash that was coming down while I was driving us home, looked like the first snow of the season. I still remember thinking, that this ash looks like snow. How can it damage a car engine?

I drove Dad back to his house while Jason and I walked him into the house, we checked to see if there was anything that I could do for Mother and Dad and then I drove the seven miles to my home. The ash was falling hard by this time, it was like a winter's blizzard only instead of it being white like snow, it was more of a gray powdery ash.

And still I thought, how can this stuff stop a car engine? He came home soon after I got home, and we stayed in the house all that rest of the day and into the next morning. When we looked out the next morning the whole area was covered with ash. We were lucky in that our vehicles were not damaged nor were our lungs. We didn't have face masks at first but then he drove over to his folks and got some face masks for all three of us. We had a puppy that we kept in the house. I remember that he shoveled paths to the vehicles. Then it started to rain, and that ash turned to a weird mud like substance. We had a lady in Troy who collected as much of the ash as people could bring her for her Ceramic Store. That spring the fields of crops became greener and greener and taller by the day. The farmers called the ash the best fertilizer as it was purely organic and fell evenly on the crop fields. That fall, we had very high yielding crops and for many years after that too. The destruction of that volcano blast at the site of the blast was devastating and killed several people and took years for the blast site and mudslide (caused by the blast and falling trees down the mountain side) to recover and vegetation started growing in these locations again. But when it did start growing again, the baring exposed dirt turned into lush green grasses, flowers, shrubs and trees. It is amazing how this Earth's natural disaster can heal and good can come out of the ashes.

Mount St. Helen's Volcano

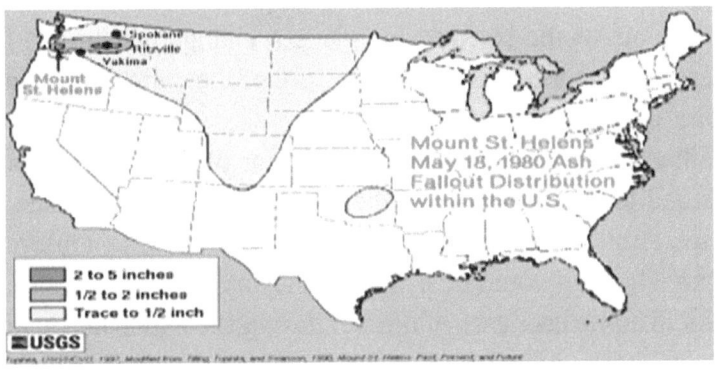

1980's- Kristal's Birth, Mother and Dad's Deaths

I waited two years before I tried for another baby, but nothing happened. Then 4 years after Jason was born, I had Kristal. Very close to my birthday. She had colic so much that it cured me of ever wanting a baby again. It seemed every evening she would cry and cry and nothing I did would stop her from crying. So, I had a wicker clothes basket that I padded with her soft blankets, put her on top of the blankets, and placed the basket and her in on my bedroom floor, shut the door, then vacuumed my living room carpet. Afterwards, I would go, pick her up out of the basket, snuggle her, change her diaper, feed her and snuggle her to sleep. She did grow out of the colic, but it was rough there for a while.

When Kristal was a little over a year old and Jason was going with his dad to ride tractors, Mother was experiencing the last months of her life, as she was diagnosed with Congestive Heart Failure. It was more than what dad could deal with so they asked their daughter Kathy if she would come take care of mother during the nights and asked me if I could come take care of mother during the days. I said yes and brought Kristal with me. Kristal was a sweet diversion for them both.

My time taking care of mother was bittersweet. My best friend was dying and yet there was something that made me feel good about taking care of her in her last days. I did not have enough time with mother, but she was dying so the best thing I could do for her was to take her care and then hold her hand. Then when I went home, I cried in the shower. Then bucked up and went out to take care of my family. I have always said that, mother gave me my life's work, in her dying. This was the very first job I ever had since getting married. It was so hard to lose mother.

Dad on the other hand, soon after mother passed away, the clinic called dad to remind him of the bill that he owed. I think it embarrassed him to no end and festered in his mind. By the time I came that day or the next day he was livid. Accused me of stealing the check for the clinic out of the mailbox and cashed it myself. That made me livid. I called the clinic and said, when that envelope and check come into the office, you'd better call dad and tell him you received the envelope and the check. Then I told dad that I would never steal any money from him and if I needed money I would ask him for it to his face, and if that's all that he thinks of me, well you can just sit in your misery. The check came in the mail to the clinic that day or the next, but it was 5 years before I talked to dad again.

One of their sons and his wife were taking care of dad before this happened, so I wasn't leaving him totally alone. But I didn't need that kind of abuse from him. Leaving dad alone didn't made me happy. Isolation from family. One day, dad fell on the bathroom floor and stayed there for 6 or 8 hours. A few days later my uncles called for a family meeting. When it was told what had happened to dad, it was asked, what shall we do with dad. At this point I was 6 months pregnant with Karen and told them that because dad was 6 feet tall and though light, when a pt. falls, its dead weight, which is heavier than the normal weight, so I can't take care of him and seriously, don't want to (I still wasn't over being accused of stealing money from him). I said that there was a nursing home that I worked at for about 3 weeks (until my husband made me quit), and that I knew personally that the nurses and all the staff were top notch and that I recommended that he go there. The next day, two of the sons took him to that nursing home.

I would go in to see him at the nursing home and he would beg me to take him out and take him back home. He made me feel so guilty. The charge nurse was a friend of mine, so I went into her office, told her the guilt trip that he was doing to me. She said, he's pulling the wool over your eyes, as he is having the time of his life with all the Canasta and Pinnacle card games that he has going, sometime two different card games a day but at least one going every day. Next time you come, sneak in and just watch him at his game. I did, and he was laughing and having the best of times. Then I showed myself as if I had just gotten there and it was the same guilt trip. I took him down to his room and spoke. "Nope. You stop this right now. I watched you. You were having the time of your life just now until you saw me. You are not going home so you'd better make the most of it. Period". With me, he stopped it, but his youngest son, dad laid that guilt trip on to him thick and heavy.

I was called by the nursing home that his time was short, that I'd better come in. I went in. I took his hand and told him that I am sorry. That I love him. He held my hand and said he was sorry too, that he knew that I loved him and that he loved me too. We both cried. Then he said, you'd better go now. My friend told me that some people don't want anyone with them when they died, and this was what dad wanted. We said our peace, now leave. Before I got home, he had passed away.

The Inheritance

B ack in the 1980's, mother and dad decided to sell their farm to one of their sons. Dad was the bank, and the son was to make agreed upon monthly payments to dad. He made a few years payments but then he stopped. Then years later both mother and dad died, and it was time to read the will. At the time of drawing up their will, they decided to write my mom out of the will, since she was "a ward of the state of Washington" and they wrote me in, in her place.

I remember when I was in grade school, they were going to legally adopt me. I remember mother asking me if I would like that and I said, yes, but could I keep my same last name? For some reason, Health & Welfare got themselves all up in mother and dad's business about having me live with them. So, to solve that problem, they were just going to adopt me. I have no idea how or why Health & Welfare dropped the case, but because they did, so did mother and dad drop the adoption of me. I was their child from the day I came to live with them at 3 years old and forever would be, in their eyes and in mine.

So, when I read the will, they had dropped mom out of the will, giving her $100. And a quilt and gave me same status as their natural born children, it slightly surprised me, yet it didn't. They gave mom $100. Because they knew that whatever dollar amount, they would give her, the State would come in and take that amount, say it was due to the State for her care. The quilt was one that mother had made for her and they knew that the State wasn't interested in that and would leave the quilt for mom.

We all were given items from mother and dad, most of which I received mine at the time of the reading of the will. Mother and dad had 8 children, and 2 of those children had passed away in their 40's because of cancer. Those two children each had 3, and 2 children of their own. Their mother's share of the inheritance was to be divided between the 3 and the 2. So now we have 8 +5 people deserving of an inheritance that wasn't in existence, but, that the will was still as binding as any legal document. It didn't seem right to me, but I didn't want to be the one to make the uncle "pay the bank" and therefore the division of the inheritance could go forth.

Several years went by, and over the course of those years, I started getting phone calls from 2 of mother and dad's sons and all of my 5 cousins all saying the same thing. "Rosemary, do something about this." I asked each of these people why me? And each of them said, "it's because you're the honest one." Thank you, but No. I am not going to be the uncle's scape goat or "Kicking Stone" so no. Finally, I said to my "husband" , then very next person who calls me I will say to them, "Okay, if you pay for the lawyer, I will go get one and do all the footwork" (thinking that hitting their pocketbook would make them say no). They said, yes. Oh darn, that meant that I had to follow through with it.

Since my "husband" is a farmer and was used to going into one of the landlord's lawyers to sign documents, I called her and made an appointment, then went in. I showed her the will and asked, is this worth going after? She read it and said, oh yes, this is very worthwhile going after. However, I cannot be your attorney as it would be a conflict of interest since I am working for one of your "husband" landlords. But my partner can take you. So, I went to his office, showed him the will and asked him, is this worthwhile to go after? He too said, yes! It is worth going after. I then asked, would you be willing to take this on, knowing that there will be family drama? He said, yes, he would take it on. And thus began a long friendship with both of the two attorneys, long after the will was settled. One of the friendships is still going strong. I called the first son (my uncle), who said they would pay for the lawyer, that I got an attorney and are you still willing to pay for him? The uncle said yes. He would be very happy to pay. Then I called the second son (my uncle), and said that I got an attorney today. That uncle said that he too would be happy to split the cost of the attorney with the first uncle. And thus began the battle.

The son (my uncle), got 2 of his brothers to side with him, and yes, I became their "scape goat" or as I always called it, their "kicking stone". Two of the brothers were like "What's mine is ALL mine! And you have no right to cause this problem!" The third uncle just went along with what the other 2 said. My attorney would call me into his office and have me read a brief that he just drafted. As I would read many briefs, I would silently thank Anna Marie for teaching me how to read, and interestingly thank my "husband" for making me only read biographies and true stories, and thus helping my mind comprehend facts. I did form my own decisions on yes or no for that particular brief, but I also asked the attorney, what would you do? And why? He would tell me. Then I would say, yes, that is my conclusion too, and here is why. We did go to court; the judgment was that the uncle was to pay up so that the inheritance could be distributed among the rest of the family.

The son had to log the back end of his property to pay for the inheritance. It was during or close to the time of the logging that he had a heart attack, and I was blamed for that too. When in actuality, it was his own fault, he created this mess by not making payments to the bank. I never took that heart attack on as my problem. What I did was at the time of the splitting of the inheritance, everyone was to get a certain amount, I had the attorney drop that amount down by $5,000 each person to receive, and that amount equaled what the rest of us were to receive, went to the uncle who didn't pay the bank. He wasn't owed for it, but it was the right thing to do, in my opinion. And thus, it was paid to all of us. It took years for that uncle to talk to me again, but I didn't care, right is right and wrong is wrong. He received money that wasn't due to him.. he wasn't grateful for it. Never was. I thought, oh well, at least my conscience is clear. The follower uncle and I always talked, and the other uncle eventually came around too. I held my ground whenever there were any grumblings. Well, right is right and wrong is wrong and he was in the wrong and the law nailed him. Plain and simple.

Abortion and the Birth of Karen

F ive years after Kristal was born, I started getting morning sickness again. I thought, NOOOO… I can't be pregnant again; I just can't be. It was at this point that I wanted to divorce my "husband" and if I had another child that meant that I was stuck in this abusive marriage for another 18 years. For I believed that a child deserved to have both a mother and a father in the same home. I went to the dr. and, sure enough, I was pregnant. I was angry. I did NOT want this baby. I told my "husband" that I was going to have an abortion and he had no say in this matter. I have always been a woman who believed that abortion is the woman choice alone. That no one has the right to tell her what she can and cannot do with that pregnancy. Very wisely, my "husband" told me that whatever I wanted to do, he would stand with me on that decision.

There was a dr. in Moscow who was known for performing abortions, so I drove myself to the clinic. And drove around the block and drove around the block again. All the while I was driving from my home to the clinic and around and around the clinic block, I was thinking, of the empty chair that should have been filled with a child at Thanksgiving dinners, and Christmas dinners and Easter dinners, and the laughter that should be, but is silent. I couldn't do it. I couldn't have the abortion. So, I drove back home with the baby intact. I have always had (and still do), a talking relationship with my God. So, I said to God, "Ok God, if I have to have this baby, let it be a girl."

I came home and that night told my "husband" that I couldn't have the abortion. He was greatly relieved. It really is to his credit that he kept his opinions to himself, because if he would have verbally assaulted me with not having the abortion, I would have done it. But he didn't and so I chose to keep the baby. I was angry for 6 long months. And I kept saying to God, "Let it be a girl, please let it be a girl". Finally, the anger in me subsided and I became content with having the baby. I had no baby items as I had given away everything. My real dad and his sisters sent me money and baby clothes and items needed for the baby.

I can't remember if I had a church baby shower, but between my real dad & his sisters I was able to get all the items needed. In April, Karen was born. The very next morning after she was born, I had my "tubes tied". I told the dr. you tie those tubes 3 times so there is not a chance for another baby. He said that he actually does 3 procedures in that "tying off" so that there is no chance of a pregnancy.

Women of the church would tell me that this baby would be extra special to me. I would ask, why? And how do you know that? They would tell me that they too had an unwanted pregnancy, and that baby was their favorite. That is exactly how it was with Karen. It's not that I didn't love my other two children, but the guilt that I felt over almost not having her was ever present until several years had gone by. She and I have always been close. I had a classmate's mother say to me, and to Karen, "Oh look! It's little Rosemary." This has always driven Karen nuts because in her mind she looked nothing like me. But she did, and still does to this day to some degree.

Bread Baking

Mother always made homemade bread ever since before I could remember. I used to watch her make it, kneed it, make loaves of bread and still have some left over for cinnamon rolls. When I was newly married, mother and dad saw that I was financially destitute, they came up with a plan to help me. "Rosemary, I'm getting too old to make bread anymore, so if you bake us loaves of bread every week, I will pay you for it." I said "Ok, I can do that". Together, mother made bread with me in her kitchen, and I learned how to make it. Sugar, warm milk, salt, yeast in just the perfect temperature of lukewarm water, and flour. All these ingredients need to be the right amount and then after the flour has made the dough sort of stiff, turn the dough out onto a floured bread board and knelt until it has a perfect texture. Put back into the bowl and let rise two times, and then cut the dough into loaf size and knead one last time, place into bread pans, let rise and bake for 30 minutes, then turn over the pan so that the baked bread pops out onto the breadboard. Let cool and eat. I made bread for mother and dad for the duration of mother's life. The money I earned was a Godsend and the bread I made for my family was a staple in our lives.

There is a Bible story in the Old Testament: 1 Kings Chapter 17, about Elijah going to a widow in Zarephath. In Zarephath Elijah meets a widow and he commands her to make him some bread. She says that she only has a little flour and oil but not enough to make a loaf of bread. He tells her to go. And make him some bread and then to make herself and her son some bread. The widow did as he asked and miraculously the flour and oil did not run out.

One day I needed to make bread for my family and there was no flour. I had no money to go to town to buy flour. What to do, what to do. I looked one more time in the flour bin, and there it seemed was enough flour for a loaf. So, I started putting all the ingredients into my bread making bowl and there was the exact amount of flour for the total process of making the bread. This happened time after time. This is a miracle that happened that I still remember to this day. As my "husband" didn't put any flour in the bin nor did he give me any flour and mother had passed away when this happened, and no one came to visit me or even knew that I needed flour. God has been good to me.

1990's and My Work Life

When I was asked by mother and dad to come and take care of her during the last few months of her life, we chose to have Hospice come into her home and help with her end-of-life care. It was a rewarding time for me because taking care of an older person was different than taking care of children and a "calling" that was satisfying to my soul. I hated losing mother, my best friend, but at the same time my heart was happy. I have always felt that mother gave me a life's work in her dying. I watch how all the different people who worked with the hospice freely gave the care that mother needed. I thought, someday, I am going to work for this agency. I don't know how or when, but I am going to.

Sometime after mother died, there was a prominent man in town who needed help taking care of his wife who was wheelchair bound and needed constant care. He called a lady in the church, "do you know of someone who could come and work for me?" She said, " yes, I do know someone." I am pretty sure that she called my "husband" first, because when the guy called me, my "husband" was fine with me working for him. The lady was a lesson to be learned with. She would tell me to turn the heat up. I did. Then it was too hot, then it was too cold and so it went with everything I did for her. I was determined that she wasn't going to break me, and I stayed working for her until I had bad morning sickness with Karen, so that I finally quit. However, that taste of a second income was nice for my "husband", and so he "allowed" me to work at other jobs, with the exception of working for a nursing home. He didn't want me working "on the Sabbath" even though it is sanctioned by the church that working in the health care service on the Sabbath is acceptable to do.

I was 30 when I had Karen, and after a couple of years of being a stay-at-home mom, a lady in Moscow called me and asked if I would come in and help take care of her "husband" and clean her house. I did. And made substantial money in doing this. I would take my girls there with me and they played with her Yorkie dogs and the girls would bring their dolls to play with too. Immediately the "husband", wife and I struck up a friendship that lasted until first he died and then years later, she died.

California and the beginning of the end

My grade school through high school friend, Sandi, is living in the suburbs of Portland Oregon, and had been accepted into the Loma Linda School of Medicine, in Loma Linda, California. Because she already had a degree from college, this was a 2-year intense program in the Occupational Therapy school. She attended the first 12 months of school, then came home for a few weeks and was to go back for the second 12 months of school.

She called me one day and asked if I would be interested in flying to Portland, then drive with her down to California, then fly back home to Idaho. She would have some company and I would get to see the sites of places that I have never been to before. I said oh yes! I would love to go, but my "husband" would never allow me to go. She said, well if you pay for all your expenses (plane tickets), have your mother in law take care of the kids for just the 7 days you will be gone, buy all the lunch makings, meals made and frozen so that he couldn't complain that you left him starving, and since he is in the middle of harvest and doesn't come home until about 10 or 11 pm and leaves at 7 am, he really wouldn't miss you at all. So, if you get all your ducks in a row, there wouldn't be anything that he could complain about. I was working for the lady in Moscow, and earned the money for the plane tickets, I sent Sandi the money because I wanted her to buy the plane tickets since she knew the itinerary of the trip and the best airports for me to fly in and out of. I started making and freezing lunches for my "husband", I told my mother-in-law about the trip. She was happy that I was going and said yes to babysitting my kids while I was gone. I got my ducks in a row..... except for one thing. I didn't ask for permission to go. I had told him about this trip and why Sandi wanted me to go with her. As the time got closer and closer for me to leave, he started giving me the cold silent treatment. That is what he did to punish me. I grew so used to it that I stopped paying attention to it. Finally on the morning I was to leave, something happened to my car, (surprise, surprise… not) and I had to have him take me to the lady in Moscow house, as that is where the shuttle bus was to pick me up to drive me up to Spokane, where I was flying out of. I said, "Why are you so mad that I am going?" and he said" It's because you didn't ask for my permission to go." So I looked him in the eye and said, "Sandi wants me to drive with her down to California, can I ask for your permission to go with her?" He said, "No". I asked, "why not?" He said, "Because you didn't ask for my permission in the first place." I said," last I checked, this is America, where we are all free to choose what we want to do, even as a person, even me." Then he said, "I wanted to be the one to take you to California, not someone else." I said, "well, I am still going, so get used to it." And I did go.

This was my first time flying, and I loved it! Especially the take-offs and the landings. I still love to fly and always will. I flew from Spokane airport to Seattle to Salt Lake City and down into Portland where Sandi picked me up at the airport. There are portions of the drive that I have forgotten about but what I will never forget were these memorable places.

Ashland, Oregon was the first stop for Sandi to show me the town and the outdoor amphitheater where every summer, the Shakespeare company would hold plays. It was a fascinating place to see. I still remember seeing the wild swans swim in the pond there and sitting on the benches that are in a round seating circle with the stage up front and an aisle for the actors to peek during parts of their plays.

I had never seen the Golden Gate Bridge, so Sandi made sure that I got to see her in all her glory. She also took me to the crookest street in America. When her hair pin turns and corners, it was so fascinating. We stopped at the Ghirardelli Chocolate factory and ate at Fisherman's wharf.

Then it was on to San Louis Obispo where we spent the night, and where I had my very first ever full body massage. I loved the massage and from then on, whenever I would go see Sandi, we would get massages. The next day, we took a tour bus up to Hurst Castle. I had previously seen the Pittock Mansion in Portland. However, this castle was just mind boggling to me. It is so beautiful, so awesome. What I remember most are the marble steps, the marble statues of Greek gods and goddesses and the blue and gold tiles of the swimming pools. I now dream of having a blue and gold swimming pool.

It was in San Louis Obispo that I found in the very bottom of my suitcase a letter written by my "husband" with pages and pages of vile things he said about me and that how I was going to hell because I disobeyed him and on and on about what, I don't know because I stopped reading the letter. Sandi started laughing and said, "Did you know that you and I are lesbian lovers? And that you're going to hell because of it?" I said "What!?" and then I started laughing too. . Nothing was further from the truth. We have always been friends, platonic friends. That is all. I am sure that he didn't think I would show the letter to Sandi, but I did. Did it ruin my trip? Yes, it did because he got into my headspace, and I started having panic attacks (at the time I didn't know there was a term for it, I just called them hot and cold sweats and shaking all over my body), as to what would be happening to me when I got home. It is exactly what he wanted to have happen, so that I would be miserable and never disobey him again. Because he's told me so often that I was going to hell, I now say to people, "Won't he be surprised when HE doesn't make it to heaven either". It took a long while for me to shake it, but finally I did and I enjoyed all the rest of the trip, and that is to my credit that I could tamp him down, at least till I got home.

I remember stopping in Carmel by the Sea and the 21 Mile Golf Course and then Solvang, California. This city is a Danish fashioned in the Danish architecture with a Danish/Dutch wooden windmill among other authentic looking Danish buildings. I had never seen a town that looked so old world: Scandinavian, Dutch, and Danish looking before. I remember the awe that I felt seeing this city for the first time. Then on to Loma Linda. Before I left, she arranged a boat ride so that I could see the houses and yards of the rich and famous actors.

Soon it was time for me to board a plane bound for home. The excitement of the trip was replaced by panic attacks and dread of what was to come to me when I got home.

Rape

I boarded a plane in Orange County, California, flew into Salt Lake and then on to Spokane Airport. From there I caught the airport transit bus down to Moscow, that drove me to my friend's home, where I got into my car and drove to my mother-in-law's house to pick up my kids.

My mother-in-law was happy that I was taking this trip and was happy to babysit the kids for me so that I could go. When I got to her house, she was so mad at me for taking this trip. I took the kids home, put them in bed for it was late and Jason and Kristal had school the next morning. He didn't come home until about 10 or 11 o'clock that night. I was in bed when he got home. He said to me, I'm going to punish you for taking this trip. I'm going to withhold sex from you. I just laughed out loud on that one and said, "You're not punishing me, you're only punishing yourself on that one".

He went into the bathroom, took a shower and when he came out, threw off all the covers on the bed, pulled me down to the bottom of the bed and raped me, hard. There! That will teach you for disobeying me! And he raped me for 3 long months. I got so that to not let it get to my psychic, I would say, harder... is this the best you can do? Finally, he got tired of it and stopped raping me. But to me the damage was done. This was happening to me at a time in history when there were no laws on the books to prevent this from happening to a married woman. She had to endure whatever her "husband" wanted to do to her. Several years after this had happened to me, there were laws put into place where rape of a spouse is considered criminal, but I had no recourse in the matter, and I just had to "take it". After that, I stopped listening to him anymore. Even if, when there was a law against it, it was my word against his, and I would have been the one being dragged through the mud again, so why bother? So, I didn't press charges. Three months of rape. Shaking my head. Why didn't I leave? Because I had 3 kids in tow and no job, no money of my own, and in my heart, I knew that if I left him, he would kill me. Not sarcastic, but serious. So, I stayed. I thought, when Karen turns 18, I would divorce him, but for now, I just needed to get through these years. She was 4 or 5 years old when this all happened.

Work

I went to work for a lady in Moscow, who was my age and had severe Multiple Sclerosis and needed help in the daytime hours. I stayed working for her for about a year and a half. During that time, she had the hospital's home health come in every week to do medical work on her. The hospital had a combined home health and Hospice department. I watched and helped the nurses as they would do their medical procedures on her and learned as I watched. Finally, I started telling the nurses that I'd like to work with them in their department. They would tell me, don't go in just yet, there is a hiring freeze right now. Every week they would tell me this. Then one week, the nurse said, "Go now, into the office and pick up an application". I went in directly after getting off work from my M.S. lady. I asked for an application. The director said fill it out right now, so I did. Then she called me into the office and hired me on the spot. She had been keeping tabs on me ever since I told the nurses I wanted to work with them. I had gotten my Idaho C.N.A. license within that year that I worked for my M.S. lady and that was the biggest hurdle for me to have gotten. Once I had that license and the hiring freeze was over, I had the job.

I had much to learn, I was so green at the job, but I felt alive in this work that I did with both home health and the Hospice. I made so many mistakes, got called into the office time after time but she didn't fire me, and I didn't quit, and I learned. I have always said, and still say to this day, that I am a Hospice worker to the core of me. I worked for this department for 9 years. In my job as a C.N.A., I drove all over Latah County, Idaho, making house calls. There were 3 of us and the lead C.N.A. would divide the work equally between us, saying, I'm going to Potlatch and Moscow today, Rosemary you take Troy -Elk River and Suzie you take Genesee and Kendrick.

This is where I met my very good friend Suzie (who I became very good friends with while working for the hospital's Home Health and Hospice Department), and still after all these years later we are still good friends. One day the director asked Suzie if she would like to come into the office and work and she jumped at it. The director asked me if I wanted to come into the office to work too and I said, "No, I'd like to stay out in the field working". And so, I did. About once a week, Suzie and I would walk the perimeter of Moscow, from the hospital to the library and back, making a full circle around the downtown area. Since we didn't work out in the field together, we would do these walks and the friendship grew. The nurses could feel that I was an abused wife, and they gave me encouragement whenever they could. These core nurses, that were there when I started are still around today. In fact, Suzie had a dinner party this past summer, for those of us who still lived in the area. The youngest of the group is me and the oldest was the social worker for the Hospice, is now 94 years old. Is still to this day a sweet, sweet friend. All these ladies are special to me, 23 years later. True friendships never quit.

I have worked for many different home health agencies and one Hospice agency and none of them compared to the quality of the hospital's home health dept. 1In general, I disliked working for the agencies, and I would quit them as soon as I could. Preferring to work private pay. The rules and regulations of the insurances, Medicare and Medicaid for the hospital's all over the country made it difficult for them to keep the home health's and the Hospices that the hospitals just closed out the two dept. Which I think is a shame.

Favorites

I had a Hospice pt. that was a Navy Ship's Captain and was dying of some form of cancer. One day his wife met me at the door, crying, she said that she wished that he would just tell her he loved her. That's all she wanted. And then she left to go on a walk while I was there. While I was doing what I came there to do, I said to him... You know, I've been married for a long time, and sometimes I just want to hear that he loves me (Now, this is the truth because I hadn't heard these words out of my "husband" mouth for years). I said, that's all we want to hear.

He was quiet for a long time, then he said, you know, I'm a Captain over 5,000 men. I know men, I get men, it's women I don't get. I don't know how to say I love you. I said, take her hand, look deep into her eyes and say, I love you. She will do the rest. Also, if you can, tell her what you feel about dying. This is a hard subject to talk about, but if you can, the relief that both of you will feel is immense.

The next time I came to their home, she met me at the door, and said, Thank you. I said for what? Because I had forgotten that earlier conversation. She said "he looked me in the eyes and said that he loved me. And I cried. We hugged and we talked. We talked about him dying, down deep on a personal level. We cried together and hugged, and it was the best conversation we had in such a long time". She and I stayed friends for many years after he passed away.

When Karen was a toddler, her little pinkie got slammed in the front screen door, while I was outside picking Raspberries. She cried and cried till she was horse. I didn't hear her and finally when I came into the house, I heard her crying, stuck in the door. I opened the screen door and there was her littlest finger, basically pinched into two sections -lengthwise, with the blood not into finger that was pinched in the door. I called the dr.'s office and then drove her, and Kristal and myself to the clinic. The nurse and the doctor both said, there is nothing we can do to save her finger. Too much time has gone by with no blood circulation to the pinched part of that finger. Go home and let it fall off. I was beside myself. She's going to lose that part of her finger just because I wanted to finish picking raspberries.

I drove to a friend's house there in Moscow, who was an old country nurse, and cried while Karen cried. The friend said, she's not going to lose that finger, and today's doctors and nurses don't always know everything. She got out a dishpan and ran lukewarm water into it and poured a fair amount of dish soap into the water. Then she took Karen's hands and put them into the soapy water. Together they played with their hands in the soapy water. As the water got cool, she would add warmer water, for about 15 to 20 minutes.

Then she rinsed Karen's hands and said, "look mom, her finger is back being all plumped up". And sure enough, it was. I said, "How did that work?" She said, the soap brings the blood flow down to where the soapy water is. She said, do this several times a day until it isn't red anymore and the finger looks like all the other fingers. I did. And today, you would never see or know or even guess that she almost lost that finger.

Years later, I had a pt. who had dementia, and my job was to go and be "a standby assistant" bath aid for him. One day, he wouldn't take his socks off nor let me, but finally, I was able to take his socks off. There was a red, angry big toe. I looked closer and there was sewing thread wrapped around and around and around that big toe. I asked, why is this thread wrapped around your big toe? He said, because it offended me. I called the office and told his nurse what had happened, and that, if I had her permission, I would soak his foot in a lukewarm pan of soapy water. She said yes, go for it. Then I called his daughter and told her the same and asked for permission to soak his foot in lukewarm soapy water, and she too gave me permission.

So, I did just that. While his foot was in the water, I slowly unwrapped the thread from his toe. By this time his daughter got to his house, and she watched as the blood came back into the big toe. She added episomal salt to the water. She came twice a day to soak his feet and I did when I came to his house on my scheduled days. Together— but mostly it was his daughter, that saved his big toe. We both thought for a long time he would lose the toe, but he didn't. Soapy warm water, that's the trick.

One time early on in my Hospice career I had a pt. who had cancer. The cancer cells would grow on top of each other leaving an open wound. My job was to go in and change her wet dressings, cleanse the wound and put dry 4X4 pads back on. AKA: wet to dry dressings. I had never seen this open wound and it scared the daylights out of me. I went to my director and asked please take me off this case. Why? Because the wound scares me so bad. She said, no, you WILL go in and take care of these wet to dry dressings. This was my nemesis and when I was told to go in, ok then I will conquer my fear. The director made sure that her nurse was in the home when I was there. I did conquer that fear and it served me well, for after that anything difficult that came up, I thought, if I can do that, then I can do this. And I did.

One time I had to go in and give a guy who broke both legs and arms a bed bath. All the nurses coached me on what to expect from this guy who was my age. The director said, now major rule of thumb. Ask him if he can feed himself and when he says yes (she knew that he could), hand the washcloth and then say, ok, wash your private parts. And leave the room or go out to your car while he does. I did as I was instructed, and though he was very disappointed, he did his own washing. Not a favorite pt, that is for sure.

50 % of my job was driving the back county roads and 50% was pt. care along with paperwork (which I didn't like at all), and staff meetings. But it was the country roads and the people that I enjoyed the most. I got to really see up close all the smaller towns that make up the county that I live and work in, and one of those towns is a town that today I have chosen to live in.

One of the times that I chose to leave the home health & Hospice dept. , for a change of pace, I went to work in a nursing home's assistive living floor. It was during this time that Kristal was at Upper Columbia Adventist Academy. Her advisor wanted to take a group of students on an E.F. Educational tour of Paris and London, and could she go? Yes, she could. Her dad wouldn't pay anything for her to go, so it fell on me to pay for her trip. I paid for it all on a wage of 8 bucks an hr. But I paid for it and she went. This trip was the beginning of her globe travels, and she still travels today. She just returned from a college roommates wedding in Geneva, Switzerland. I later went back to the hospital's home health and Hospice dept. Until 2000. When it was agreed by both me and the director that I should quit.

I was assigned with a patient who was a rather large lady, and since she lived right across the street from me, I would save her for my last patient of the day. I would go into her home, do a small bit of chit chat and then we would get down to the business of why I was there. I had been going there to see her for several weeks, when I was just about ready to leave, she said, "Rosemary, please sit down. I want to have a talk with you." I did sit down.

She said, "If I were to grade you on your work, for me, I would be giving you an A+. You do your job very well. But If I were to grade you on your sincerely caring about who I am, and what I have gone through in my life, I would be giving you an F. You see me as a very overweight woman who is on Medic aid and living in a poorer condition than what you live. I know how you live because you live right across the street from me. You have never asked me about my hobbies, not once have you asked me what my life was like before coming to your town, you have no real empathy for me. Oh, you do your job well, and that is the extent to your being here."

As she talked, I hung my head in shame. She was right. I had no defense. None. I looked up at her and said, "You are right. I am so very sorry. Yes, I am ashamed to say that by not talking with you, I treated you less than I should have. From the bottom of my heart, I would like to apologize to you, and honestly ask for your forgiveness for the way I have treated you."

She did forgive me, and to this day I will never forget that "talk" that we had. Because I opened up my heart to her and asked about her life, and what brought her to this point in her life, I found out that we had similar situations in our married lives. I asked her about her hobby of crocheting and her love of fine thread crocheting compared to my yarn thread crocheting and that I hated fine thread crocheting, I asked her if she would crochet me some fine thread Christmas tree ornaments and she did. I asked her later if she would crochet me a piano top tablecloth and she did. I paid her for all that she did me. I would walk across the street and visit her after she was discharged for home health, and I was sad when the moving van came to move her to another location.

The lesson that all this taught me was this: do not take people who are living with Medicaid assistance to be a less person than myself. That I have no idea as to what their life was and is like that has brought them to have to rely on federal government assistance. That someday, it probably will be me.

I said that because I have chosen to work for either in home care agencies or preferably private pay, in home care. For working for agencies, the pay was 7-8 dollars an hr. If I chose to take the $8. An hour then the agency would not pay for their share of my insurance. But if I chose the 7 dollar an hr. wage, then I would have their share of the insurance cost, but the pay was at a lower rate... it was a catch 22. I did go to college later in life, but I dropped out during my junior year for various reasons. And now in my later life, having to go on Medicaid assistance myself because of working for agencies at low pay. That lesson learned so long ago has been driven home to me in full force, into my face. What we humans do to make the less feel even more less. Shaking my head.

2000-The Divorce and how Old Man helped me

$\sim$

I n the late nineties, I started house cleaning for Old Man, and every time I would go there, we would talk, and I would tell him how my married life was going. He said to me that you need to leave him, I said, yes, I know that I do, but I'm afraid to. Afraid that he will kill me. Old Man said, I used to belong to your church, and I know just how to get him to let you go. I said, how? He said just never mind, but know this, your reputation is going to be ruined so if you can handle that then you will get your freedom. I said, yes, I can handle that. But he wouldn't tell me his plan. Old Man asked me to fly to New York City with him to visit his niece who lived there. I said, I can't go with you, if my "husband" wrote this epistle of a letter to me, gave me the cold silent treatment and then raped me because I went to California with a grade school girl friend, then think what he would do to me, if I went to New York City with you, a man.

Sometime later, my car broke down at Old Man's house and my "husband" went to Old Man's house to fix the engine. Old Man walked outside his house and stood beside my "husband" and said… (and I will use his exact words here), "I'm fucking your wife, she's going to divorce you and marry me." The next morning, I was getting ready for work and my "husband" came into our bathroom and said, "SO! Your fucking Old Man, huh? I said "What? What are you talking about?" At that moment I knew what Old Man's plans were. The panic attack happened to me instantly for his voice rose higher and higher and got this pitch to it that only happened when he was … mad beyond mad.

Later that day I went to Old Man's house and told him what had happened, and Old Man said, you need to leave him now, before he kills you and get the divorce started. Very long story, most of which I have forgotten but I did not go home that night. I stayed with Old Man in the other half of his house with a bedroom, bathroom and living room all to myself with a shared kitchen. Old Man said we should get out of "Dodge" for a while, so we drove to the Oregon Coast. Two Motel rooms. Then a week later, we came back to Moscow. I called a lawyer, and the divorce proceeding began. It was not an easy thing to obtain. The one thing that his lawyer and him concocted was that because my mom was mentally ill, that meant that I was too, and they petitioned the judge to have all, and I mean ALL my medical records sent over to his lawyer's office, and it was granted.

I want to tell all of you who are reading this, that the governing HIPPA, that protects anyone from knowing, reading or hearing of your personal medical information is NOT covered when your medical records are subpoenaed by the court and the judge signs off on it. You have no protection from HIPPA. When it was all said and done, the lawyer and he read completely through my records for any mental illness and found none. But that doesn't mean that I wasn't angry that they got away with it.

In fact, later, I moved out of Old Man's house and into my home, where my "husband" moved into his mother's house. Then very late at night, he would walk from his mother's house to my house and take a tree branch and run it on the side of the outside of the house. Other times he would get up on the roof of the house and walk on the roof. It was a double wide with the outside walls being 2X4 thin and every little noise he made could be heard. When this first started happening Sandi and I were talking on the phone, I was in bed with the light out when the tree branch started being rubbed and ran around the outside of the house. She could hear what he was doing on the outside of the house, and we listened together. She heard him walking on the roof, through the phone. She is my proof that he was trying to gaslight me into thinking that I was going crazy. I wasn't.

One night he wanted to take me to see the new house that his brother and him were building, (I was staying at Old Man's house at that time), and Old Man said to me, you'd better not go with him, because this is where he will kill you if ever he is going to. He said, be careful, because he will try to grab you while you are still in my house, but I will stop him. I said "How are you going to stop him? You're an old man and he is a muscular man". He got a golf club that he always kept beside his chair, and with both hands threw the golf club up in the air and caught it and threw it several more times. I asked how that is going to stop him? And Old Man said, a golf club can break any bone in the body and especially the skull, and your soon to be ex knows this. When he came to get me, and tried to get me to go with him and I wouldn't, he tried to grab my arm and that is when Old Man took his golf club and threw it up and down in the air, and when he would leave, Old Man stood up and leaned on the club and he took off out the door. I am pretty sure that he stalked me at Old Man's house that night and most every night since I left him.

When our 25th anniversary came, I said to my "husband" that since we never really had a honeymoon, I'd like to go to Hawaii and he said, I'm not paying for it. If you want us to go, you will pay for it. And that was the lynch pin that drove me to leave. This was in June, and I waited until after Christmas to leave him. When I moved back into my house, he would come over to the house to repair things I had asked him to repair for years. For example, the kid's bathroom particle board floor. He wouldn't do it before but now suddenly, he was there to replace the floor. Then one day he said to me that he will pay for the vacation to Hawaii. I said, nope, too late, you should have said this to me last year and then done it. Nope. I will not ever go anywhere with you again. I am divorcing you and there is nothing you can do to stop me.

One time, during that time I was living in my house and he was there to "fix something, he hit me, and I grabbed a pot of last night's leftover soup and hit him with it and dumped the content of it over his head and said, DON'T you EVER hit me again, because I will hit you back harder than you have ever hit me! And to his credit, he never tried that again.

It took about a year and a half (2001.5) to finally have the divorce granted, and when it was, I didn't know or care because the day I left him, in my mind, was the day I divorced him. For a couple of years after the divorce, he tried to woo me back, and one time as we were hugging goodbye, he whispered in my ear, if you ever come back to me, I will make you pay, for shaming me. I unhugged him and looked him in the eyes and his face was blank, like he never whispered those words. Friends- that is gaslighting at its finest. Now really, why would I ever want to go back to someone who just told me they would do hard to me? And I never have gone back to him.

New York City

I left him in January and started the divorce proceedings soon thereafter. In the summer of that year, Old Man again asked me to go with him to New York City, because now I had left him and didn't have to worry about what he would do to me. But I still didn't really want to go to N.Y.C. so I told Old Man that I would go but only if I could do 3 things while there. 1. I wanted to see a Broadway play, 2. I wanted to see Ellis Island, because my biological dad's mother came through Ellis Island and 3. I wanted to see the Catskill Mountains. He talked with his niece, and they agreed to all three. So Old Man and I flew from Spokane Washington to LaGuardia Airport in New York City.

It was on these round-trip flights that I would look down on the "fly over states" and wonder what life was like for them down there. Twenty-three years later, I would take a long dream of driving across America, those "fly over states" and see for myself the very long and flat and farmlands and big cities of middle America. Driving from Idaho to Pennsylvania and Vermont and then round trip driving back to Idaho. Dreams, they do come true.

Old Man's niece and nephew in-law met us at the airport in a stretch limo with a driver. We saw all of N.Y.C in the stretch limo for all seven days that we were there. I did get to go to an off Broadway play at the Shubert. The play was in Chicago, which was better than the movie they made several years later.

His niece lived in Sleepy Hollow, and they drove us around to see the Roosevelt mansion, The Vanderbilt Mansion, and a few other famous people's homes. They drove us around downtown N.Y.C, showing us the beautiful architect. We were most impressed with the twin towers. Old Man and I took a horse and carriage ride around Central Park, we saw Wall Street and many more downtown sights. We drove in the limo to Mystic Seaport, Connecticut by way of the Catskill Mountain freeway.

At the time we went to N.Y.C., the HBO show "The Soprano's" was in the middle of their seasons, and I loved watching the show. There were things that the niece and nephew did or had, that reminded me of the show. One being that they had a store for just beer. And every morning the niece would count the money from the previous day and night till. Very much like the Soprano's.

The most interesting thing that I got to see, and they all were so interesting, but it was Ellis Island that I will never forget. My grandmother's name is etched on a wall outside of the building commemorating along with others who have immigrated to America, by coming through Ellis Island. It is a vast building with tile walls museum all around the building. His niece and nephew had been to Ellis Island and weren't interested in going on the tour, so they sent the limo driver to go with us.

I hadn't eaten breakfast and in the middle of all the walking, I had a low blood sugar attack, and the driver went to the employee's dining hall for some orange juice. He said, "Don't move from this spot!" Ok. We won't. But Old Man wasn't about to "stay put" and started walking around. The place is so big that he could easily get lost, and because he wouldn't sit where the driver told us to sit, I had to go with him because I was afraid, we would never find him. Finally, the driver found us, he pulled me aside from Old Man and said, "You didn't stay where I told you to", and I explained why. Then he said, "if ANYTHING had happened to you, or especially Old Man, his nephew would have me killed." The terror in the driver's eyes told me that he was serious about being killed. It was then that I knew that the nephew was in the mob somehow, someway.

It was one year later that the twin towers were taken down by two airplanes. I was getting ready for work when the news came. Old Man called me on the phone, "Are you seeing this?" , "yes". And we cried over the phone together. Just a year before, we had seen those beautiful buildings, and now... all the lives lost, and the beautiful buildings gone. I am so glad that I said yes to the New York City trip. All the experiences I would have missed if I had said no, I want to stay in my little corner of the world and not venture out and just be in my bubble. Anyone who knows me, knows that I am up for adventures and this N.Y.C. trip was an adventure that I will never forget and so glad that I said yes.

Narcissistic Person

I feel that it is important to list some of the signs of a narcissistic person and the signs and symptoms of Post-Traumatic Stress Disorder so that if you should experience either of these, you can be aware of what is going on and get help.

1. Having an unreasonably high sense of self-importance and requiring constant.
2. Excessive admiration.
3. Feeling that they deserve privileges and special treatment.
4. Expecting to be recognized as superior even without achievements.
5. Being jealous, possessive, and controlling of their partners.
6. Blaming others for their problems and never taking responsibility.
7. Cheating, womanizing, and manipulating others.
8. Gaslighting and making others doubt their reality.
9. Being preoccupied with their self-image and appearance
10. Being preoccupied with the weight and appearance of their wife, girlfriend and children.
11. Having sexist ideas about women and their roles.
12. Being charming and charismatic at first, then turning sour and abusive.

PTSD

Post-traumatic stress disorder symptoms may start within one month of a traumatic event, but sometimes symptoms may not appear until years after the event. These symptoms cause significant problems in social or work situations and in relationships. They can also interfere with your ability to go about your normal daily tasks.

PTSD symptoms are generally grouped into four types: intrusive memories, avoidance, negative changes in thinking and mood, and changes in physical and emotional reactions. Symptoms can vary over time or vary from person to person.

Symptoms of intrusive memories may include:

- Recurrent, unwanted distressing memories of the traumatic event
- Reliving the traumatic event as if it were happening again (flashbacks)
- Upsetting dreams or nightmares about the traumatic event
- Severe emotional distress or physical reactions to something that reminds you of the traumatic event
- Negative thoughts about yourself, other people or the world
- Hopelessness about the future
- Memory problems, including not remembering important aspects of the traumatic event
- Difficulty maintaining close relationships
- Feeling detached from family and friends
- Lack of interest in activities you once enjoyed
- Difficulty experiencing positive emotions
- Feeling emotionally numb
- Being easily startled or frightened
- Always being on guard for danger
- Self-destructive behavior, such as drinking too much or driving too fast
- Trouble sleeping
- Trouble concentrating
- Irritability, angry outbursts or aggressive behavior

- Overwhelming guilt or shame

Forgiveness

———— ◠◡◠ ————

After I had moved out of my married home and into my own solo apartment in the town of Troy (I stayed in Troy, for it was my hometown and I wasn't going to let him push me out of MY hometown), I drove to visit Sandi in the suburbs of Portland, Oregon. While there we went to the movie, The Passion of Christ. I was so moved by this movie, thinking that if Christ could forgive those who crucified him, then I could forgive my soon to be ex.

The next time he came to visit me at my apartment, I looked him in the eyes and said: "I want you to know that I forgive you for all the things you did to me." He said: "Why would you forgive me? I didn't do anything to you." I stood on my tippy toes and got in his face and said: "I knew that you would say that, I was there when you did whatever it was that you did to me, and I remember what you did to me, and I still forgive you." And I did. For you, you see forgiveness as not so much for others, though that certainly is important, but it is for you, within yourself, to become free of anger and bitterness. You don't have to forget, but it is God's law to forgive with an open heart. I forgave and the anger started leaving me.

We in Hospice, we tell the spouse to give themselves one month for every year that they were married or together. For instance, they were together for 2 years, that equals 24 months, to grieve. However, for me, I was married to him for 26 yea (when I was all said and done), so, it should have taken me 26 months, when it took me around 15 years to get over the abuse that he inflicted upon me, and our children.

I am now the happiest that I have ever been, but I am very aware of people who try to hurt me mentally, I will always turn and walk away from them. My life is too short to deal with him and them ever again.

Salzburg, Austria

I n 2000, Kristal started her first year of college at Walla Walla University, in Walla Walla Washington. One of the reasons she chose that college is that when a student takes a year of foreign language, the college will sponsor that student in the country of their chosen language. Kristal chose to take German language because that is what her dad's heritage.

For her sophomore year of college, the school sent her to a small town just outside of Salzburg, Austria, since they don't have an affiliated college in Germany. She started school in the fall and at Christmas time she called me and said, "Oh mom, you have just got to come over here and see this beautiful country." With my tax return money, I bought a round trip airline ticket to Salzburg. Interestingly, when Kristal flew over, she flew to New York and then around the world, and when I flew, it was to Spokane then to Seattle and then up over the top of the world. When we came home, we each flew the same routes we went over on (roundtrip tickets bought), and got into the Spokane airport just minutes apart from each other.

She still had a few days of finals to study for and then take, before the end of school in June, so while she studied, I slept off the jetlag that hit me hard. She toured me around the area on a college student's budget, meaning, we walked everywhere or took the train when it was too far to walk. She took me to the castle at the top of the city, named Festung Hohensalzburg. Most of the time she took me everywhere "The Sound of Music" locations, as she knew that I love that movie. At the top of the castle, I could see the Austrian Alps, and could easily see the pass where The Von Trapp family was supposedly walked through and over the Alps. Close to Kristal's college there is a smaller castle that is a Duke or Earl's castle and is so very beautiful. We ate lunch at an outdoor café and saw the large fountain of water where the Von Trapp children sang, "doe Ra Me". The lane that Kristal and I walked from the town of Salzburg back to her college dorm reminded me of the lane where the children hung upside down in the trees. One day we were walking back from town, and we walked past a white house up on a hill. She whispered, "mom, look to your left, see that house up on the hill?" "Yes." "Mom, that is the childhood home of Adolf Hitler." It was the creepiest feeling ever to see his home, there in this beautiful city. The streets really are small and tight, as in a Mini Cooper would just fit perfectly, but no American cars or SUV's. The country roads, on the sharp corners, have large round mirrors on posts so that you can see around the corner, to see if anyone is coming. Sometimes I think American roads need these round mirrors too. Another thing I experienced was my first round about. I was so impressed by how the cars all knew when and where to go. Nowadays, they are prevalent, but in the early 2000's, not so prevalent.

One day we were shopping in the small shops in the piazzas, when off to one side and out of the way of foot traffic, there is an outdoors's chest board that is 4 feet square for each square and is white and gray checkerboard. The pawns are made from balsam wood that are painted white and black and each are the shapes of the proper chest pieces. At the top of each piece is a large round ring that the people can use to move the pieces from square to square. I am still intrigued by the outdoor chest board and pawns. I'd like to have one in my own back yard, someday.

On this same trip to town, while we were walking in the piazzas, it started to rain and then it down poured and everyone scattered into the shops. While Kristal and I were running, a man stopped us and said to me, "let me cut your silhouette picture". I said, "No, no, no... my nose is too long, no. "He said," I can make you beautiful." So, I let him. He took his scissors and black paper and snip, snip, snip, and when he was done, he had cut out a picture of my mom, in one of her prettiest professional pictures. I such in my breath, said "you got this from my side profile?" He shook his head ,yes. I paid him very well for the picture.

I love their round alley doors. They are old, wooden, and rounded at the top of the doors, like in Robin Hood or King Arthur's day. Again, someday, I'd like to have a round door. The cobble stone streets that one walks up or down a steep hill. And the shops, mostly Christmas tree bulbs for sale all year round, with Mozart chocolate balls. Their everyday chocolate bars are smooth and silky tasting. It took me a long time to want to eat Hershey's chocolate bars again. Their grocery stores are different than ours with less food or variety on the shelves, but they were adequate.

The buildings are each a different color. In Salzburg the colors are pastels or orange next to pinks, next to greens next to blues next to browns next to yellows next to whites. I think they must have a paint ordinance for they all were uniform and spaced out in the colors. Other towns have bright bold colors in the same color wheel. I took a bit to get used to it, but I can imagine that they think the same of American's bland concrete or brick colors. The sidewalks and the buildings are so close to each other that one could feel claustrophobic if a person was inclined to be that way.

She took me to see Mozart's home and museum. Impressive, not only his home but how he composed music at such a young age. And the contemporaries too, like Beethoven and Chaplin.

On Saturday night, Kristal and all her college friends took me out to a German pub to have pizza. This pizza was like no other pizza that I ever had before. It had red sauce, and then on that there were fried potatoes, fried parsnips, and other unusual vegetables. Unusual looking but oh so good. Even the parsnips, which I am not fond of.

I stayed in her dorm room with her for the 7 days that I was there. On Sunday her dean of girls drove us into Salzburg where we caught a train that took us to Vienna, where we caught our different planes home to Idaho, USA.

College

Back in the 1990's I wanted to go to college to become a nurse. I asked my husband if I could go, and he said no and got really mad at me for even thinking of going to school. Telling me that I was too dumb to even be in college. Towards the end of 1999, I brought college FASFA's home and asked him again if I could go and would he help me fill out the forms and again he said no and threw an angry temper tantrum. So, I thought, well I will just wait until I divorce you and then I will go. It took me three or four long years after I divorced him to get my head back on straight but when I was 46, Sandi helped me fill out the FASFA forms and I sent them off in the mail. Then Suzie basically took me by the hand and walked me around Lewis-Clark State College, in Lewiston, Id.

To tell you the truth, I was scared out of my wits, because I didn't know if I could even do this thing called college, but how would I know unless I tried. If I tried and then I failed, well, at least I would have tried. I was talking with my advisor about what classes to take and we decided that I should start out easy by taking just the prerequisites courses for college. While we were talking, a man came into her office and she introduced us. I told him how I was scared to take any math courses for fear that I would consistently fail them. He said, "Well, I happen to know your math instructor and I am pretty sure that he will pass you in every class you need to take". Turns out, he was the math instructor.

When school started that fall, I was enrolled and became a full-time student, while working, taking care of a lady with dementia. I would go to her either before my classes 30 miles away, or after. In that math class I would go to work, then drive to school usually being late for class about 5 minutes. Soon it got to be a "thing" where the other classmates would make bets as to how many minutes, I would be late. One day, a gal who used to babysit for me when she was in high school and was in that math class and I went to lunch after that class. I asked her, the kids in that math class seem to treat me differently when I walk in the room than before I walk into the room. She asked me what I thought of the kids, I said, "Well, they are my own kid's age, so I think of them as my kids". She said, "Good because they all think of you as "mom". And if you can make it to class even though you're working, then they can make to class too. And if you can do the work, and get the grades, then they can too. They, especially the guys, are working extra hard at getting their assignments done so that you're not "showing them up". Have you noticed that when you get stuck on a problem, there are 3 or 4 guys willing to help you?" I said, now that you mention that... yes, I have noticed it and have wondered about it." She said, they all like you and want you to succeed and that makes them successful too." One day we had an open book test, and I had this perplexed look on my face, the instructor asked me what was wrong. I said, "I've forgotten what pi is". And from around the whole room, there were15 different voices that told me what pi is. By the way, it is the ratio of the circumference of a circle to its diameter, or 3.14

I had to take at least 3 different English classes. I remember one of those classes, freshman straight out of high school were in this class and then there was me, a middle-aged woman. The instructor wanted to get us out of our (or their) clicks so she would pair us up, assigning 3 students to a group. She put me in with my most dreaded group of girls, and I am sure they felt the same way about me. The assignment was to write a description of a place that you like to go to, to be alone. I wrote about how I would get off the school bus, go into the house, change clothes, grab an apple, and walk a half mile up a hill to "my rock". I described the rock in detail and told how I would write letters to my boyfriend who was in college in another state. Then she had us switch essays with each other, and then we had to read the other person's essay out loud in class. When mine was read out loud, the whole class was quiet and after that reading, those girls became my friends, on their volution. The instructor knew that if those girls could know the real me who was a high school girl just like they were, they would change their opinion of me, and they did. Through all my college days, we were all friends.

One day that same instructor said to me, "you need to teach English." I said "oh no, no, no, . I don't even know what a verb, or noun or any other names for the sentence structure is." She said. "Your teaching this class every day and you don't even know it. She said, "you watch today, you'll see." The emails were not new, but still new, and so she said. "When you send an email, you just start in with the body of the message." She let that sink in for a bit, and then she was watching me… and I spoke up and said," back that troller up a bit", and from around the room, heads came up, pencils down laptops closed, and she looked at me with her eyes cocked in that..." see, I told you so, she smiled and we had the most interesting conversation between her, me and other students. After class she said to me, "See, I told you so. You NEED to be a teacher. "I smiled. But you know what? It was because of that instructor that I had the courage to write my first book.

I was taking a class in Human Biology, and I totally enjoyed the class.

The problem was, at mid-term, I was flunking a class that I "got" or understood. I went to my advisor and said, "I'm flunking a class that I understand. I know that it is a learning problem, I want it figured out now! As I don't have time to waste." I was sent to a learning psychologist at the University of Idaho. It was there that I took a battery of tests, and it was determined that I have adult ADHD with a major learning disability in math and science. Science, the heart of the classes I needed to take. I eventually dropped all my nursing classes for a Social Work degree, but my grades slipped so much that in my jr. year of college, I dropped out of school completely. I have always said and always will say, that going to college was one of the best things I ever did for myself… (well, that and getting the divorce). The psychologist prescribed Strattera for ADHD. And it helped for a while, but then the side effects were worse that the benefits, so I weaned myself off the medicine. I had an abnormal Psych instructor tell me that drinking coffee does just as good as taking any medicine, and I think that it is true. To this day, I am a coffee drinker, especially if I want to accomplish anything that day.

I earned enough credits to have my Bachelor in General Studies, but if I couldn't have my nursing degree, or even my Bachelor of Social Work degree, then I wasn't interested on the general studies degree. In Idaho to make any money with a social worker's degree, one must have a master's degree. I always thought I might go back, but, probably not. I make just as much money doing my private pay in home elderly care as I would with the B. of social work.

In my very first Social Work class, we were required to watch the movie, "One Flew Over The Cuckoo's Nest". At first, I couldn't watch it because my mom spent her basically her whole adult life in a mental institution and I couldn't bear to see what she had to endure. My professor very gently convinced me to watch it.

Finally, I could. Thank God that it was Jack Nicholson as the main character, with his humor, but it really was Nurse Ratched, that was the villain of the movie. I got through the movie, crying all the way through it. At that time, AMC was showing the movie in two different formats, I was regular, the other, was having footnotes running at the bottom of the screen, explaining why and what was going on. For me those footnotes were a lifesaver, as it helped me see clearly what was going on.

I was able to hand in the class assignment and then one day the professor showed the whole movie in class. Thank God I had watched the movie at least 3 or 4 X's already, so in class, I could eat my popcorn (yes, he did have popcorn, he was a pretty cool professor-social worker himself) and get through the movie unemotional. I would have to say that this movie is one of my all-time favorites. I am saddened by the news, that Louise Fletcher, aka: Nurse Ratched, has died. Instantly, I was transported to when I was 47 and having to watch the movie for that first time. Yes, I did hate her, but she did her acting job well, for she won an Oscar. :)

My Biological Dad

When I was a little girl, my dad would write me letters saying that he would be coming to get me on that next Saturday. Mother would read me the letters and I would be excited to see him. Come that appointed Saturday I will be dressed in my best Sunday dress and shoes or sandals and wait for him at the wooden bridge gate. I would hop on the gate and ride it back and forth, all day long, waiting. Looking down the road, waiting. Soon the time came and went. Well, maybe I got the day wrong, so the next day I would dress in my Sunday dress again and wait and look and wait for him, but he never came. He did come to get me, twice that I remember. I remember both times that he stopped at a tavern in between Troy and Moscow, called Dirty Ernie's. I remember that one time he let me go in with him, other times I had to wait for him in the car. We went to his mom and dad's where my grandma made fresh banana bread and my grandpa let me go down to the basement to get a large bottle of 7-UP. Then after an hour or so, he would take me back to mother and dad's, stopping at Dirty Ernie's on the way there.

In college I took a class that helped me understand what was happening with my dad. You see, he was an alcoholic and when he would write me a letter, he was either drunk when he wrote it and when he sobered up, would not remember that he had written the letter, or vice versa, he was sober when he wrote the letter and sent it, then getting drunk again and forgetting all about the letter. That it is the nature of the beast.

When I was in school, the letters stopped all together. On his account or mother's account, I never knew, just that I didn't hear from him again until I was a senior in high school and about to get married. He wrote me a heartfelt letter and I, in response, wrote him a scathing letter pouring out all my anger and hurt telling him just what I thought of him. He accepted my letter with good graciousness and replied with tenderness and thus the slow beginning of our relationship. I invited him to my wedding, but only as a guest. That my grandpa that I lived with and who was always a dad to me who have the privilege of walking me down the aisle. My dad and two of his sister's, my favorite aunts, came, and by their own choice sat in the back of the church.

It was a slow progression of a relationship, writing real letters back and forth and once a year I would take my family to downtown Portland, Oregon to see him. After my divorce, I had an attorney friend who told me that I needed to have my dad sign Power of Attorney papers for when he could not take care of himself. I drove to Portland and tried to get him to go with me to his bank, only to have a Notary Republic witness him signing the document. It was more than he could handle. It befuddled him and he became agitated and paced in the apartment. I left the document with him, saying that he really needed to do this signature before too long. He did take the document to the bank, had them look it over, they told him that this was a good thing for him to sign and that it would help take care of him in the future.

Fast forward to my college days and I was studying for an exam one weekend when my phone rang. It was a doctor from a hospital in Portland, close by where dad lived. He stated that my dad fell down some outdoor steps and broke his clavicle and abrasions on his face. Could I come to see him? The exam was the next day, I stayed, took the exam and then drove the 7 hours to Portland. My friend Sandi and I went to see him at the hospital, and he was in bad shape. Long story short, Sandi and I found a rehab. Skilled nursing home that would take him in the town where Sandi lived. Then after he became better, Sandi and I found a private elderly group home for dad to live in. He lived there for a couple of years when he died of suspicious reasons. I wasn't there at the time of my dad's death but suspiciously, the owner/director vacated all the residents of the home and had emptied out the house of people and furniture and left some of my dad's stuff on the porch. It was the strangest thing I have ever encountered.

I had bought a chair for my dad for this group home. I wanted this chair for my own home when I was loading up my dad's possession, interestingly, it had a stain in the back of the chair. I thought, well I can just shampoo this chair and make it look good as new. Sandi and I loaded it up in her pickup and left it in her basement until I could come back and get it. It had strange vibes to it and made Sandi's company feel awful, like something sinister was associated with the chair. Sandi called me and we talked about it, and I asked Sandi if she and her "husband" could load the chair back up into the back of her "husband" pickup and haul it to Good Will. They did. Putting the chair in one direction. When Sandi got into her pickup the very next morning, the chair was turned in the totally opposite direction. She couldn't drive fast enough to Good Will to get rid of the chair. To this day, it gives both of us chills to talk about it, so we rarely do.

All the years of dad's severe alcoholism caused him to have an alcoholic Alzheimer's Disease called Wernicke-Korsakoff Syndrome. This happens due to the lack of thiamine. This essential vitamin converts sugar into energy. When you have too little thiamine the brain doesn't have enough energy to work properly. This deficiency is chronic in alcohol use. Also, other causes for this syndrome includes:

Poor Nutrition is caused by non-eating or eating disorders.

Chronic Infection

Weight loss

Head injury – his falling on the outdoor steps and hitting his face hard on the sidewalk.

Confabulation – Where the person invents information to cover memory loss. This is a BIG tell-tale sign.

Confusion and disorientation. The confusion makes it difficult for the person to realize that anything is wrong and seek treatment for medical problems.

Balance Problems or loss of Coordination and unsteady gait or walking

Heart issues

Lack of muscle coordination- Ataxia

Eye Issues

Amnesia or the inability to form new memories.

Behavioral Changes such as agitation or anger

Again, Confabulation

Each symptom could be symptoms of other dementia problems but when I rolled all the years of alcoholism and then each one of the symptoms combined, it was an Ahh Ha! moment for me, making things up and his anger outburst towards me for no apparent reasons, started making sense to me.

When he died, I talked with the director of the funeral home, and he helped me get dad a full military service and burial in the Portland Military Cemetery.

I had called one of dad's sisters and asked if she could call other family members, and I tried in vain to find my brother to tell him, but I could not locate him, but in the end, it was just Sandi and myself who attended his funeral services. Since it was just Sandi and me, we decided to go somewhere funky for the funeral dinner. We decided to go to Hooters. Yes, it was rather sac religious place for us to go to dinner but considering all that we had been through dealing with dad, it seemed a rather "interesting" send off for him. Sandi was with me for all the 17 trips from home to Portland that I made from the first fall in March until college started in September, making sure that dad was well taken care of. Then all the anger and confabulating's of his making up facts that were not even close to the truth, for the weird way his care provider of the group home left, basically in the middle of the night, why not do something off the wall for the funeral dinner. Did I press charges against his care provider? No, I didn't. Not for lack of trying, but since she left in the middle of the night, there was and still is no way of finding her. Once dad had died, in my mind, it was the end of a not so happy era with him, and I just wanted to be finished with all the dramas of him.

My Biological Mom

As I have already written, my mom was committed to the Eastern State Mental Institution in Medical Lake, Washington, just outside of Spokane, WA. From the time I was a little girl, and came soon afterwards, (having spent a short time in a foster home), to live with her parents, "mother" and "Dad". When I was a little girl, mother and dad would drive up to Medical Lake and bring my mom home for Thanksgiving and Christmas. The institution is a white brick building that to me as a little girl looked like a grand mansion. I remember riding in the back seat of the car, looking at the building and saying out loud that "someday I'm going to live there". And mother in a very indignant voice would say, "Oh NO you won't!" I would go into the building with mother, to get my mom for the 3 or 4-day visit home with us. I remember bars on the windows and doors and arms of women "inmates" reaching out to touch me, a little girl. It scared me so bad that I remember that scaredness to this day. I remember my mom looking "different" than most people and that she acted "differently" than most people too. It was all so confusing to me, to have this woman who was supposed to be my mom be more like a child than an adult. I won't go into all the things I remember about her, more out of respect for her and that I have chosen to forget as much as I can about those days. But it was as a child of a mentally ill person, to see and hear and feel all what I did as a child. And then, to have to go back to school and be taunted by other school kids about my mom. Some traumas can never be undone.

When I was in high school, I did research on what happened to people incarcerated in mental institutions. When mom was committed into the institution, for what should have been diagnosed as post-partum depression, was instead diagnosed as schizophrenia. Thus, shock treatments were the norm for those diagnoses. Although, it seems that most people in the institution and my mom was no different, receiving shock treatment as the norm. She received the 1950's through the 1970's high dosages of the electroshock treatment, on an ongoing basis throughout her stay there. The movie, "One Flew Over The Cuckoo's

Nest" is a very real depiction of life in the mental institutions. And a movie that was very hard for me to watch (being a required movie to watch for a Social Work degree class, but once I was able to get through the movie, I was then able to watch it a second time during the required class time).

In the mid 1970's the wisdom of the United States government decided that all inmates in the mental institutions throughout the United States should be turned out of the institutions and into the streets. And thus, we have mental illness people who are homeless and with no place to go after living so many years in the institutions, who are forced to live in the streets and homeless encampments of today. This time period is where that all started, with the so-called wisdom of the government. Do I sound bitter? You bet I am! The institutions, under the guise of making mentally ill people better, instead made them basically non-functioning people. And this was the case for my mom.

In the mid 1970's I was married and had a young child and scared to death of being force by the government to take my mom in and take care of her for the rest of her life. This was a very real fear, for I had NO idea as to how to take care of someone who the institution destroyed and then… "here! YOU take care of her!" Her mother and dad were too old to be taking care of her and that is why I was afraid that the care would fall on my shoulders.

Mother and dad received a letter from the state of Washington stating that when the time came for my mom to be let out of the institution, they would assign a Skilled Nursing Facility (SNF) in Spokane, WA. to take care of her for the rest of her life. What a relief it was to both mother and dad (her parents), and me (her daughter). She would stay for several years in one SNF and then was handed off to another SNF, and so it went on for the duration of her life.

One day, I was at work when I received a phone call from my mom's doctor telling me that she has died. She was 65. Her doctor told me that she died from heart failure. That basically because of all the shock treatments she had to endure throughout her life, she died with a heart of 95-year-old woman. Am I bitter? Yes, I am. I would LOVE to give those so-called doctors a good healthy dosage of the same volts of shock treatments that they gave her. My heart is still very sad for her. It wasn't fair. Not even the remoteness of fairness to her. I am still so very angry at everyone from her mental institution. How I would love to sue the pants off all of them. Things that happened to her in her life weren't fair. An abusive alcoholic "husband", 4 babies in 4 years with a miscarriage of one of those babies, being institutionalized at such a young age in her 20's, the death of a young child, none of these things were fair to her.

I had a grave side funeral service for her, and all her brothers and sisters and all our families came. She is buried in our family plot in a country cemetery outside of Troy. I sincerely hope that she gets to go to heaven for here on earth, she lived in hell for the better part of her life.

Underhand and Deceitful

I once had a patient that had specifically asked for me to come to help his wife take care of him. I had known him and his family since I was a little kid. In his later years of life, he went to the same church that I used to attend. I liked his wife and kids a lot, but he tended to scare me, so when he asked me to come take care of him, I was very much surprised, and a bit intimidated by him.

One day, after several months of my working for him, he said, "Sit down, I want to have a heart-to-heart talk with you." Okay??? So, I did. He asked me, "Have you ever wondered why you can't get any jobs?" I had a surprised look on my face because yes, I seriously had been wondering why I couldn't get any jobs. I said, "How did you know that's what I've been thinking?" He said, "Before I answer you that, do you use the hospital as one of your work references?" I said "yes, I do. I Left in good standing with them, and they told me I could use them as a work reference." He said, "so, have you applied for jobs and gotten any?" "Yes, I have applied but no, to the jobs."

He said, "You need to go the H.R. department of the hospital and ask to look at your personal file." I said, "Why?" He said, "I'm not going to tell you why until after you go look at your personal file." I never did go, didn't even want to go look in my file. Finally, he said, "okay I will tell you why. This is what he told me.

"You know that I go to your church?" "Yes, I know, you started going just before I divorced and then left the church." "Well, because I am hooked up to an oxygen machine, it makes noises during the church sermon, so I go out into the foyer and sit in one of the chairs out there and listen to the sermon over the P.A. system. I am a short, old man that nobody pays any attention to. One day, your ex and his buddy who is big wig in the hospital come out to the foyer and start talking, hatching this plan- against you. Well, I looked like I was listening to the sermon, but I really was listening to them. This went on for several weeks, but they finally came up with a plan… the big wig would write a cover letter saying, "Don't hire Rosemary because she had sex with her patients. And that he would place this cover letter in the very front of your personal file. Now Rosemary, I am telling you… Get yourself into the hospital and take that cover letter out." "Rosemary, in all the time you have been here with me, you never even flirted with me. I have known you your whole life, and I know that this is a falsehood in the biggest proportion. GO! Take that letter out of your file."

That very afternoon, I did go into the hospital's H.R. department and asked to see my file. The assistant happily got my file out of the drawer, opened it up, and there, front and center were that letter. She wouldn't let me see my file, saying, hum, I need to get the director of H.R. They took my file into his office, and soon, I heard a paper shredder going. After they had shredded it, they brought my file to me and acted pleasant, I took one look at my file and said, "Well, I'm glad it's gone." And closed my file and handed it back to them. If I had actually seen that letter, that would have been a lawsuit just waiting to happen. That's why they shredded it.

The next day, I went back to my patient and told him that he was right. And what happened at the H.R. department. He said, "Damn right, I was right." He said that wanted to tell me, but the only way he could do it without their knowledge was to hire me to help take care of him. I am so glad that he told me, and that I did something about their deceitfulness. When I stopped working for him, and started applying for jobs again, I was hired with no problems after that. This patient and his wife stayed friends with me until the end of their lives.

Why would the ex and the big wig do this to me? Well, to get back at me for having the audacity of divorcing him and to make me so financially broke that I would have to come crawling back to him on my belly. I never did. The ex-needed someone who could move around the hospital, and no one would question why he was there. That's the big wig.

Gaslighting

About 10 years ago, a guy that I have known for my whole life, asked me to go out with him. I said No. No. No. One day he called me up and said, "I have something that I want to tell you, but it's going to take me a long time to tell. So, how about if we go for a long drive, somewhere for lunch and I will tell you what I want to say." I said, Okay, but this is NOT a date, ok? Ok.

He said you drive while I talk. Okay. He said to me that he wanted me to do two things. One. Put my thinking cap on and two, Remember way back in time. Okay. So while I was driving he said to me, "Did you know that your "husband" was having an affair with my ex-wife, while the two of you were still married?" I turned and looked at him with my mouth falling open. He said, "Now this is where I want you to go back in time, and put your thinking cap on, and remember. And then he was quiet. All the while, the memories came flying back to me in vivid colors. "OH MY god!" Then he said, "You know that baby she had. That was a miscarriage?" "Yeahhh.." "Well, that was his baby. A boy." I said, "now it makes sense to me, soon after the miscarriage, I took flowers to her house, and she wouldn't see me. Then one day I saw her at a store, and I said that "I am so sorry that you lost the baby", and she said with stink eyes, "WHY WOULD YOU CARE THAT I LOST THE BABY?" That statement finally made sense to me, in all the years, it never made sense to me. And now it does.

He said, "I would be driving up to get to my kids from their mom's home to take them to school and there was your ex's pickup, either in front of her house or up the street a few blocks away. I asked my kids about that, and they would say, "oh, yes, he's always here." I just turned and looked at the guy telling me these things. I didn't know that he was going there in the mornings, but he would point blank tell me that he was seeing someone. At that point in the marriage, I didn't care. But now, finally, it all was making sense to me.

It was at this same time that my ex would accuse me of having an affair. I wasn't. It was the furthest thing from my mind. When I married,

I married for life. But after all the years of him accusing me, I finally did let an affair happen. I did have an affair. Not with anybody that anyone knew about. And certainly, not Old Man, who my ex always thought it was him. And I did tell the guy in the vehicle with me about my affair, long after the miscarriage. This is not something that I am proud of, but as with being told "Who would ever date you, you're so fat you could never get a date even if you wanted to." I was out to prove him wrong. And he was wrong, because I asked to get married at least 3 times, but I always said no. Thank you for asking me, but no.

The guy in the vehicle also told me that his ex-wife said, I can take her "husband" away from her any time I wanted to." I said, "well, I wished I would have known that, for I would have thrown him at her, saying Here! Keep him. I don't want him."

This and I can count 3 other affairs my ex had while he was married to me, and yet, I was the scarlet women, and everyone felt so sorry for him.

This miscarriage memory has brought to my girls and myself ahh ha! Moments, as to why he would not be as high up in the church as he was. A Lot of things started making sense to us." Ahh, no wonder why......."

At the end of the drive and luncheon, I was drained, but it was good to have things start to make sense. As it did with my patient who told me about the letter in my personal file.

Dating a Man Who was a Closeted Drug User

Many years ago, I dated a guy who, unbeknownst to me, was a severe drug & alcohol abuser. He hid it very well from me, until I started noticing things, for ya know, you can't hide a bad habit for very long before it comes to light, and that is what happened. Finally when I'd had enough and was about to turn and walk away from him........ His dad came up to me and said, you're going to leave him aren't you? I looked at him, and said yes, I am. How did you know? I haven't told anyone that I am. He said that a woman has a look in her eyes when she's about to walk. He said to me... when you do leave him... for absolutely for good, I wonder if..... you would give me a chance? I said but, but, but, his dad. He said yes, I know I am, and you can slap me if you want to,, but I feel and think that you and I have much in common. I said, but you are his dad and you're 20 years older than me. He said, yes, I know. but if you would give me a chance, I can make you very happy. I said, welllll... you're going to have to do all the pursuing, because, I'm not going to. He said, deal.

Ever so slowly he started reeling me in, slow and then he kissed me. The chemistry was there, that wasn't there with his son. I slowly fell in love with him. I said, why me? he said, I fell in love with you almost from the start of you dating my son, but kept it to myself, for I knew you would dump him once you figured out his demons, and you did.

We had so much in common, and my love for him grew. I totally gave him my heart.

He had a bad heart, and one Sunday he was transported to a heart hospital in Spokane, Washington. He called me to tell me that his end was soon coming. His son and I drove up to Spokane. His son said his good byes to his dad, and then went out to the parking lot/ car to get a drink. While he was gone, I told the man that I loved him, deeply. He said that he knew that and that he loved me too. He said, I will meet you at the gate(can't remember exact location, but he gave specific location), he said that he will be waiting for me, no matter how long. I watched as he coded and the team of doctors and nurses did CPR on him, but his heart blew out.

I sat at the nurses' station, numb. The son and I drove home. No words were said between us.

Then, I started getting pennies from heaven. The song, Bridge over trouble waters came on the radio, no matter what station I was listening to, always, . and then about a year later, when my heart was healed, the songs stop playing on the radio.

I have a medium that I started talking with about that time when the songs stopped.

I wanted to talk with my grandparents about a decision that I needed help with. I said that I also want to talk to this man. She said, he has been standing just outside the door, waiting, hoping that you would want to talk with him. I did. I asked, was I just in this love, or were you too? He said things to the medium that only he and I knew he said to me. Yes, he still loves me deeply.

So, that is my love story. my kids thought that I was going crazy because I always talked to him and spoke of him like he was still alive. In my heart, he is and it has been him ever since, that I am so content to be single.

I just wanted to tell you my love story, and to know that I know what true love does feel like and if I find someone now, he has a lot to measure up to. I am not opposed to being in a relationship, but, I'm not interested in a booty call but rather in true relationship.

The Meth heads above me

T wo married kids moved into the upstairs apt. above me. He was leaving her in January, telling me that he couldn't take her abuse anymore. In February, she went to Kansas to see if she could live with him there. She couldn't and came back here, telling me that they had a knock down drag out physical fight, she came here, and he went to Spokane (or so she told me, whether that's the truth or not remains to be seen). That very week that she came back, she moved to her new boyfriend into her apartment. Right above me. And that is when all the problems started.

The unbearable noise started from day one, and I would call her, tell her, you want to stop the noise or should I call the cops. Many times, I would call her. The noise didn't stop. The slamming of doors and stomping and dropping things on the floor. Then, the nighttime noise started. One night, then it became a regular event, they are keeping me awake all night, dropping barbells or crank shafts, slamming dresser drawers, dropping boxes on the floor. I had to work at the hospital's Covid Vaccination clinic the next day. That day, we worked a full 8-hour day putting through 550 people. Midway through the morning I got physically sick because of lack of sleep. I called the chick and said that because they kept me awake all night that I was now sick, and for them to stop then noise at night, if not then I will call the cops. The noise the next night got 100% worse.

Every time I pay my rent to the caretaker of the apts. I complain about their drug infested noise. He just shrugs and says, "There is nothing I can do about it." For my April rent, I called the caretaker & had him come to my apartment. He sat in a chair by the fireplace. I told him how the kids upstairs (the chick 23 going on 12 and her boyfriend the same age), were driving me to a breaking point (nervous breakdown) and that he needed to do something about it, or that I would have to move because I just can't take this constant noise, dropping things, slamming all kinds of doors ALL THROUGH OUT the night. He said, "Let me see if there is anything I can do to stop them from being noisy. He didn't.

The housing market is tight in this college town and there was no place for me to move to, so I was stuck there. Plus, a stubborn streak hit me and I thought: I will not move from here, because these drug infested kids want to bully me out of here.

That day, about an hour after he left, the chick ran the vacuum, and cleaned & aired out the house, and the garage door opened & closed, in what I suspect he was putting the barbell or heavy objects that he drops repeatedly during the nights. I thought, hum… funny how they are cleaning their house right after the caretaker leaves, when they haven't vacuumed since the boyfriend moves in.

Several times, I have verbally voiced on the phone or in person conversations in my apartment, things about the upstairs kids and their drug activity and every time, that night, the noise would increase exponentially, to an unbearable noise level. After talking with the care taker and hearing her cleaning and airing out the house, I began to wonder if they have a small microphone hanging down between their fireplace and into my fireplace, because this stuff happening is just too coincidental. Same with my verbalizing of things about them… Then—The morning that I FINALLY had enough, and I called the cops, and said, don't bother coming here in the daytime, but yeah, don't be surprised that I should call you 10:30 or 11 or later tonight. Suddenly, she vacuums the floor at 8 am, and the washing machine runs for a couple of washes, the garage door opens and closes. Coincidentally? No, I think they heard every word that I spoke on the phone to the cops. Too many times have things "coincidentally" happened. So… I know they were hearing what I was saying out loud.

Before the kids moved in to the apt. above me, I had lived for three years under the lady who lived in the apartment above me, the same lady that the quad-cities drug task force sent away to Federal prison for meth trafficking. She always made sure that she had fans on and blew the smoke out the window into her yard of the house/apartment. But I heard strange things living under her, like fans running all night all year round (she told me that she needed the white noise of the fans to sleep, and I believed her), the vacuuming her whole apartment at 3 in the morning, I knew that was a drug vacuuming up cleaning. So, when these two kids above me start their all-nighters and couldn't sit or lie still for longer than 15 minutes, I know without having to see it with my eyes that they were doing drugs.

The young couple had a little girl, who was 3 years old at the time. This little girl runs around their house with hard soled shoes. The apartment is carpeted so why the hard soled shoes? The chick kept the possession of their 2 dogs. And the dogs get all revved up and jump around and run the full length of the house when their humans come home. This never happened when the husband was still in the house. The noise level in my bedroom makes me always wonder how can that little girl sleep through all this noise? Unless…. They are giving her something to sleep?

The kids upstairs waited till they figure that I was going to bed, because there is no noise when I go into my bedroom earlier in the evening. None. But when I did go to bed, I'd turn on my TV to a level that lets me go to sleep. Usually around 11pm. I always have had a TV on to go to sleep. I have asked the lady and then the young married couple if they could hear my TV. And always, they said no. I said, "Can you hear me snoring? No, we don't hear a thing". And I never heard a thing - while the husband was there. I never even heard them have sex. Never.

And then the new boyfriend moved in. OH my god! The noise from the bed is unreal. Now I like good sex, but this is not good sex, and it's being done to make me stay awake. Like I said, I never heard it when the husband was here.

Then there was the noise from the squeaking floorboard that is right above my head bed and by the window, they like to sway back and forth on that one board, knowing that I can hear it and keeping me awake.

So, starting about 11pm and going clear throughout the night till they finally fall asleep, the squeaky floorboard, at the window and at the entrance to their bedroom, dropping boxes and heavy stuff, boots. You name it, they drop it. Sex, loud talking (never ever heard them talking to each other when the husband was there). Once, while they were out of town, at 4:45AM an alarm clock went off solid until 9 AM. Never had an alarm clock before this, or after, but now I know that this was a new nerve grating thing to happen when they were out of town.

The husband lived in Spokane, and every Monday, Tuesday, and part of Wednesday, the chick and her boyfriend are gone, Monday and Tuesday nights are the nights when I can get a good, deep night's sleep.

Then it starts all over again. Except for the alarm clock going off one night, all night long.

I suspect that while they are in Spokane, they replenish their drugs (meth or crack) because the noise is so constant- like a roar- constant, and by the time, it's time for them to leave again, the noise level has come down- a bit. In March, I told the caretaker of the house that their pot smoke was so thick, that if I stood still in it and breathed deeply, I could have gotten high off of their second-hand smoke. He did nothing about it. In Idaho It is a crime to smoke pot.

Many years ago, I had moved up to Silver Valley to be closer to my aunt & uncle for a short time. I rented a house, cute little thing, but what I didn't know was that this house in Kellogg, Idaho was a meth house. They manufactured it there, sold it there. I would get horrible headaches from that house. I am not prone to headaches. But I sure did get them there. Then, when the neighbor told me how nice it is that I don't have people coming at all hours of the nights, & why, I went to the sheriff's office and asked him what I could do to get out of this meth house. He said, well, ya didn't hear it from me, but if ya just don't pay your rent, they will kick you out. So, that's what I did. Why am I telling you this? Because I know that meth headache. I used to get them that last year that the lady lived there. I thought, naw, she wouldn't be smoking or using, would she? Yes, she did. So, when I tell you that I get horrible headaches now, in this house with those two kids living above me…. I know what I am talking and what is causing this type of headache. When I get these headaches, is exactly when they are smoking it or using it.

At the end of March, the new boyfriend was out in the driveway buffing her SUV and then his car. I took my car across town to gas up, and while gassing up, I noticed that the passenger front tire was low. I drove the car to Les Schwab's to fill it up. The tire guy said, "Your tire is basically flat, and the valve stem is broken. He fixes the valve stem, and the tire is fine. These tires were new as of this past November. There is NO reason for that 1 tire to go flat. Maybe just a coincident…. But still?

I needed to get a different vehicle, but I was afraid to, for fear that he will tamper that vehicle. I found an SUV that is what I want, but had to back out of getting it, because of this fear.

One day, at the beginning of the week, she had taken her SUV to somewhere, he was at home. There is a stairway that when this house was built, the stairway is between the kitchen and basement. Then it was made into apartments. Two doors, one on the upstairs apartment locked and unable to open, and one on the other side of that door, on my side, locked and unable to open. This day that she was gone, there was a MOST awful cigarette smell in that stairway. Now, I grew up in a family that smoked Camel Cigarettes, and this was even worse smelling than Camels. I keep my food pantry in the bottom few steps of that stairway. Oh My God! Are you kidding me! So, I got a tub & tile caulking, and on April 15, while they were gone, I climbed my stairs up to that door, and calked that 1" gap of space between the door & the floor. I did tell B. about the smoke smell, and he did nothing about it, so- I did.

Why didn't I report this much sooner? These kids were ten toes to the line of justice, but not over, just enough to try and drive me crazy. So, if I call the cops and say they are walking too loudly. OR… they are dropping things on the floor, or their bed is squeaking too loudly, or they are talking too loudly? Each one of these things make me sound like a nosey old neighbor or a "Mrs. K." from the old TV show, Bewitched. Who is going to believe me? But now, they have escalated to going from just one of these things a night, all night long, to doing ALL these things, ALL night long. Trying to get me to leave. Because they heard me say to the caretaker that I can't take any more of it (later I found out that there wasn't written up a rental lease agreement contract, so there is nothing that the caretaker could do about the drug problem or evicting her out).

Then, sometime mid spring to early summer, the chick started have men up into her bedroom and I would hear them having "headboard, headbanging sex". The neighbors across the street would say, did you see how many men she had has up there last night, this morning and right now? No, I can't see who goes up her front steps, but I sure can hear the headbang sex. The neighbor told me that she would come out to take her garbage can to the street dressed in what he described as "hooker" costume. One Saturday I counted 6 guys in the space of 6am to 10 am. Then she and the last guy slept all day. The previous lady's son came and moved all of her stuff out of the garage that the chick and her husband agreed to store for her while the lady was in Fed. Prison. The chick didn't wake up at all during all the noise that loading 3 trailer's loads of stuff out of the garage but woke up in time for the first of 5 or

6 more males to come to her front door, staying for 15-45 minutes and then leaving and the next guy would come just 5 minutes after that guy left. I took pictures of those 5 guys, standing in my doorway with my canon camera.

One Sunday, early in the summer, I came back home to find one motorcycle parked where I park my car in the driveway, and the second motorcycle parked in the middle of where the chick parks her car. It was done intentionally, to keep me from parking in my driveway spot, so, I drove my car right smack between the two motorcycles, wanting to hit them both, but I am too good of a driver and missed them both. The biker dudes were watching me from the window of her house, came out mad as hell. I said, "Don't Park in my spot again or I will hit it next time and I won't care". The kid said, "I won't! Please don't hit my bike. The dad came at me with words. The chick called the cops because of the verbal confrontation with the older dude. I told the cops, nope! I'm not taking this. You go do your job and get this meth head and prostitute out of here. I stopped counting how many times I have called the cops because of the meth, the noise after 11pm, 12 am, 1 am and so on. The chick wouldn't answer her door when they would knock, and the cops would just leave. I stopped calling after at least 7 or 10 times. Drug abusers and prostitutes in Moscow Idaho have more rights than long-time, law-abiding citizens do. Now, the older biker dude is living with her at nights. The neighbor across the street told me that an older man comes to visit the chick and stays 15 -30 minutes, several times a week. This last week, he walked down the street where he was parked, and biker dude was in the driveway, so the man turned around and walked back to his car. He did this about 2 more times, then he walked right past the biker dude and up to her back door, stopping to text on his iPhone, then went in. The biker dude didn't look up or do anything, but finished what he was doing and drove off. The older man came out about 15-30 minutes later. And then another guy came to the back door. The neighbors see it all. I wrote all this in a formal letter and mailed it to the Prosecuting Attorney for him to do something about it. Nothing happened. The law said that their hands were tied. The chick and her boyfriend knew all this, which is why they kept harassing me, trying to get me to move. I wouldn't be pushed out of my home that I was living years before the chick ever thought of living there.

It was at this point that the chick took her prostituting to other locations and since she was still in the upstairs apartment, the only conclusion I could come to was that she turned States evidence and snitched on her fellow drug traffickers. Finally, she moved out in November. When I toured her apartment, I saw that she and her meth head boyfriend had cut in her bedroom drywall and pulled out all the fiberglass insulation between the outside wall studs and the drywall, right above where my bed was. A large enough hole that they could blow the smoke down on me while I was sleeping. This proved that I wasn't crazy like the caretaker tried to convince me that I was. He didn't convince me; I knew what I knew. It is for this reason why I never try to speak to the caretaker again. My cousin told me that the chick and her meth head boyfriend were trying to get me hooked on the meth so that I would come buy from them. As it turns out, I am very allergic to the meth and other drugs that they were doing, and I would get violently sick.

Before I close out this chapter, I'd like to add documented effects that meth has on people, animals, houses and land that have been in direct contact with it.

Symptoms of Meth Exposure

Even years after a building has been occupied by those producing or smoking meth, there are toxic particles that remain if the duct work and building have not been properly decontaminated. Meth exposure symptoms are similar to those of other respiratory illnesses, so it is important to test for meth exposure if you notice multiple symptoms after moving into new home.

Possible Symptoms of Meth Exposure

1. Watery, red, and burning eyes, often accompanied by discharge and pain
2. Skin irritations, redness and rashes
3. Chest and/or abdominal pain and diarrhea
4. Chronic sneezing and coughing and shortness of breath
5. Negative effects on the central nervous system
6. Congestion of the voice box and other throat problems
7. Moderate or severe headaches
8. Dark-colored urine
9. Rapid heart rate
10. Yellow jaundice
11. Fever
12. Decrease in mental capabilities
13. Hallucinations

If you leave the area for an extended period of time and the symptoms subside, there may be reason for concern. Even small amounts of meth exposure could trigger symptoms. Previous use of the building for a meth lab or even just using meth near the building can cause damaging health effects. The sooner you discover meth exposure, get treated and have the building professionally decontaminated, this will lessen the risks for further exposure. Traumatic Cleanup & Restoration is professional trained and certified to aid you through the entire cleaning process.

Effects of Meth Exposure in Pets, Adults and Children

"Many of the precursor chemicals used to manufacture methamphetamine are highly toxic, corrosive, and/or flammable… In addition, many of the chemicals used in methamphetamine production are restricted by Occupational Safety and Health Administration regulations, which require that hazardous materials teams clean up methamphetamine lab sites. Reports indicate that at least five pounds of toxic waste are generated for every pound of methamphetamine produced (Governor's Office of Criminal Justice Planning Guidebook, 1999). This waste is commonly disposed of in backyards, dumpsters, storm drains, parks, or along roadsides and farm fields, where it is a source of long-lasting and toxic pollution." (Read full article http://www.ncbi.nlm.nih.gov/pmc/articles/PMC3029499/)

"Children who live in home-based methamphetamine labs are exposed to the toxic precursor chemicals, waste, and filth associated with methamphetamine production, as well as to the highly psychoactive stimulant itself. Psychoactive compounds can cause psychosis, seizures, and death from accidental ingestion (NIDA, 1998; Perez, Arsura, & Strategos, 1999). Consequences of exposure to the toxic precursor chemicals can include poisoning, burns, and lung irritation; damage to the liver, kidneys, heart, brain, and immune system; cancers such as lymphoma and leukemia; bone marrow suppression resulting in anemia and increased risk of infections; and developmental and growth problems (Drug Endangered Children, 2000; Irvine & Chin, 1997; NIDA, 1998)."(Read full article http://www.ncbi.nlm.nih.gov/pmc/articles/PMC3029499/)

HOW METH WORKS IN THE BRAIN

Property Changes

Drug activity of any kind including meth, whether use, creation, or processing often will take its toll on the property. Specifically, in trying to suss out if a meth house has sprung up, look for the following.

1. Hoses hanging from the windows (used to ventilate the house) and other modifications to ventilation.
2. New security system installed without your permission.

3. Excessive signs such as no trespassing, private property/beware of dog signs.

4. Above normal amount of garbage:
    1. Garbage and clutter about the property.
    2. Increase in garbage service/number or size of bins.
    3. Complaints or observation that occupant is putting garbage in neighbors' containers.
    4. An unusual amount of trips to a shared dumpster.

5. Newly covered or blackened windows.

6. Signs of external property neglect such as dead grass from chemical dumps and stained soil or concrete.

Suspicious Signs and Activity

In addition to changes in behavior and property status, look out for the following suspicious signs and activities.

1. Complaints of strong odor by neighbors or unusual chemical, almost sweet odors during inspections.

2. Frequent, short stay, and odd hour visitor traffic.

3. Increased utility usage.

4. Interaction with unknown persons/occupants other than the tenant who signed the lease.

5. Empty chemical containers and odd or bulk items such as paint thinner, lye, freon, acetone, iodine, hydrogen peroxide, sulfuric acid, phosphoric acid, and ammonia.

6. Unusual items of quantity such as rubber hoses, duct table, bottles and containers, pressurized cylinders, camp stoves, fuel containers, propane tanks, and respiratory masks.

7. Large amounts of cat litter in a pet-free property or property with few cats.

Additional meth use and production signs and information can be found here: National Institute on Drug Abuse | Methamphetamine

PREVENTION

There is truth in the Benjamin Franklin axiom, 'an ounce of prevention is worth a pound of cure'. But in the case of dealing with a meth lab in your rental, it's worth far more than a pound. Crime prevention goes hand-in-hand with the landlord responsibilities and this list should help you combat the establishment of a meth lab in one of your rental properties.

Better Times

B efore Covid hits in the United States, I was working in Pullman Washington, taking care of an older lady, who was in her late 80's, and was a retired professor of quilting. No, it wasn't called quilting but rather something to do with textiles. I asked her if she would teach me the fine art of precision quilting. She told me the secret is just 3 basic things. Measure correctly, cut with a rotary blade for precise cutting and iron after each seam. That's it. When I interviewed for the job, she had up on a quilting frame a design called "The Pinwheel", that she was hand quilting. With her small needle and thread and her own hands. When she finished it, it was beautiful. There is something special knowing that the quilt, any quilt for that matter, was hand quilted.

The fabric for her quilt was 100 % Civil War Reproduction fabric. Back in the civil war days, they would boil flowers and weeds to get the colors that they wanted. Then they would dip the cotton fabric into these dyes. Blue Cornflowers were boiled for the color of deep dark blues, and so on. These fabrics are appealing to both men and women as the Civil War era did not have frilly colors but rather, practical colors and prints.

A few months after she hired me, I started a quilt called "The Kings Highway". She told me, do not try to match your colors and designs. But rather, put the strangest colors with each other. For example, put purple and orange together. I said, "Really?" She said "Yes, when the quilt is put all together, the final look to the quilt with be beautiful." This is just what I did. Strange designs and colors with ones that don't match each other. I finished that quilt and showed it to my girls and Kristal said, "oh Mom, this is a very beautiful quilt, can I have it? I didn't think she would be interested in having it. I gave it to her. Then I started another quilt, my favorite, "The Pinwheel". And when I finished that one, Karen said, "Mom, it's so pretty, can I have this one. So, I gave it to her. One of the cool things about learning to quilt from this lady was that she had a type of quilting book that is very much like food cookbooks. In that these books have the step-by-step process in sewing and putting together the quilts.

This lady had a niece who stopped by for a visit who was from the East Coast of the United States. I asked her so many questions. Did you drive all by yourself? How much did cost you to drive across America? Were you afraid to do this solo? This niece planted a seed in my mind, that I would love to do this myself. She told me that she budgeted 5 thousand dollars, I thought, I could do this, and soon it became one of my bucket list items, to drive from Idaho to Vermont and Maine and back. I could do this. A couple of years later, I have the money saved up and the current job was just ending, I will do this, and then Covid hits, and shut down all of America. So, I, along with the rest of the people around the world, hunkered down in my house and baked bread and learned to be content. The money I saved went to the business of living as no one was hiring anyone for anything.

My Trip to Pennsylvania and Vermont

In recent months, I finally was able to take that trip across the United State. I was going to go solo because I knew that I could do it. I had bought a SUV specifically for this trip and I had money saved up for the trip again. But so many of my friends said that I needed to have someone with me. So, I asked my youngest uncle if he wanted to go with me. That if he did, I would have him drive us through the big city of Chicago. That I wanted to stop for a few days in Fond du Lac Wisconsin to see the birthplace and childhood home of Mother. He said that he did want to go.

My cousin Susan had come out from Pennsylvania for a visit, and I asked her if she would want to drive with us from her state up to Vermont. She said yes that she would like to do this. The reason for Vermont as my destination is that I wanted Susan and me to meet our 2nd cousins. So, with much planning we set out on our trip. The actual trip was a disaster due to problems with my uncle. A wise women told me once that if you dwell on the negative, it will overshadow the positive. So, for just that reason, I'm not going to write about the disastrous trip. I asked Susan to drive from her house to Vermont and back to her house, and to do that work for me, I paid for all her expenses.

Meeting our cousins for the first time ever was such a treat. Susan and I fell in love with them at first sight. I loved the time spent with them and the time I spent with Susan. It was way too short. The fall foliage was just beginning to show her splendor in the colors of oranges and yellows and reds. Such a treat to see these trees with my own eyes. To see the very old and still in use covered bridges and the Amish Barns and roadside vegetable stands. I had my very first ever soft pretzel from one of these stands. It was so good. Next time, more soft pretzels. I also bought for myself a blue and white "Wedding Ring" Amish Quilt. That is such a treasure. Seeing the horse and buggies and mostly women driving them was so cool.

I drove uncle and me back to Idaho cutting my vacation trip short by 2 weeks, but Susan has invited me back, only this time to fly, solo, and spend a couple of weeks sight-seeing all the places I wanted to see and spend time with family that I didn't get to spend the first time back there. I want to see all things history, and especially the Civil War Battlefields. Soon, I will be going back.

Genealogy or Why I did the Ancestry.com test

For most of my life I have been around genealogy of one sort or another. Way back when I was in grade school, dad's sister, Aunt Barbara Gilder Allen, made a Gilder family tree. This tree is filled with branches and tree trunks that look like they don't split into more branches. I never was interested, in fact I had that glassy eyed look that said, oh god! Shoot me now! I don't care about who begets who. It was like reading Genesis 1:1.

Then about 5 years ago, Sandi said to me, "Rosemary! You should do the Ancestry DNA test. It will be fun!" I said, "No, it won't be fun, and it is something that retired "old" people do. I will do it when I'm 65." Well, 65 came around faster than I ever thought it would. As in, never. But here it came. So, in May of 2021, I ordered it. The kit came and I did the spit test and sent it off in the mail. At the end of August, when I did turn 65, the results came to me through email.

At first it was fun to see what my nationality is, for I knew that I am 50% Norwegian, but wondered if Ancestry would say the same. At first the report came back that I am 51%. Huh? How do you get 51% but as I worked the lineage down through the ages, it came back to a solid 50% Norwegian. Then Scotland,24%. Then Sweden & Denmark,13%. Then England and Northwestern European,11% and Germany, 2%. I have read Aunt Barbara's genealogy report and have the old fashion pedigree tree drawn with names printed on the side of the branches. It is so confusing! But it did help in the thought of, "Oh! This family uses the same first names repeatedly. Father's, son's, 1st cousin's, 2nd, 3rd, and on down the line of cousins all have the same 3 or 4 names. In fact, someone in the Gilder linage wrote a post that says, "This is all so confusing!" I was so glad to read this because I am just about give up, but persisted on, and I'm glad I did.

When I bought the spit test, I paid for 6-8 months' worth of membership to Ancestry.com In October, I got to thinking, well I should utilize this app (This app will expire on December 11, 2021. So, I should just get started). At first it was fun to see the first few closest generations to me. But then I got to thinking, I wonder just how far back does this Gilder linage go? Who were these people, and what was their lives like? Years from now, I would want to know how this person's story fits in the linage, so I printed off the "who begets who pages and their short life's story bio page. Then, if I could find factual stories about the person, I printed that off too and put it in my notebook. I had this very naive thought that I was going to find family physical traits that run throughout the family lines. I did not find that at all. However, what I did find was-who these men were. I say men, because women, basically were there to have children and run the house and having children. Did I say, having children? Yes, a great example of that is in the Gilder linage, there is a man who has 30 children. Grant it, he had to have 3 wives- each having 10 children apiece, to get those 30 children.

Logically, I decided to start with **Glen Gilder's** side of the family. And was able to take that line out just as far as it would go. Then I went to **his mother, the Kegley line**, and took it all the way out. Then I went to Mother's side of the family. **Agnes Devereux-Clark, Gilder**, The Deveraux linage, I was always told that there is royalty in the blood and that they have a coat of armor that goes along with that royal blood. Little did I know (not at all), that all **4 linages have royal blood flowing through the blood.** But what surprised me the most was the linage of the **CLARK family**. All four linages go all the way down to the 1500's. Impressive considering I thought that if I got to 4 or 6 generations back, (1800-1700, maybe) I would be doing good, but was able to go to 11-12 Great, Great, Great Grandfather/Mother down to the 1500's and the other countries mentioned in the 4th paragraph.

How did I start looking? Well, I started with myself (Rosemary), then going to my mom (Carol), then going to her father (Glen), Maternal Grandfather, and then to his father (Robert) Maternal great grandfather, and then his father, and then his father, and so on down the line.

Interestingly, the Kegley side has twice the number of pages than the Gilder side and the Devereux/Clark side, though just as important royal linage about a third of the pages.

Then I went to my grandmother's side of the family.

Mother (Agnes), gave me a hope chest that her father made for her before he died. But that was all I knew of him. Just who was this man who was her father. His name was **Edgar Jesse Clark.** He was born in 1860 in Wisconsin. He had a lung problem and his family decided to move to this area. He died in the hospital in Bovill, Idaho not from lung problems but rather from cancer of the intestines. If you take a trip through the town of Bovill, on the main street, going out of town towards, Clarkia, on the right-hand side, on a hill right by the highway, is a big, what use to be white painted building that was the hospital where he died. He was a furniture maker by trade, and he made this hope chest for his daughter Agnes (Mother), right before he died. She gave it to me when she was 65. And now, I am 67. I have not even talked about her mother's side of the family. But, on her dad's side of the family, the Clark(e), there are some interesting people.

My English Heritage along with the Mayflower and the 13 Colonies

I n the CLARK linage, a most interesting person showed up. Now remember, that women didn't hold any office, or power, but they did marry, and Abigail Marvin Clarke married very well. She lived from 1674-1730. She was my 7th Great- Grandmother.

When Abigail was born on September 15, 1674, in Farmington, Connecticut, her father John was 37 and her mother was 34, she married Joseph Talcott in 1693 when she was 19, she then married Joseph Pixley and they had 10 children together. She died in 1730 in Great Barrington, Massachusetts at the age of 56.

Joseph (Gov.) Talcott
1669-1741, Husband of 7th great- grandmother

When Joseph (Gov.) Talcott was born on November 16, 1669, in Hartford, Connecticut, his father, Lieutenant-Colonel John was 38 and his mother Helena was 36. He married Abigail Marvin Clarke and they had 2 children together. He then married Eunice Howell Talcott and they had 7 children together. He died on October 11,1741 in his hometown at the age of 71 and buried there.

Joseph Talcott (governor)
Joseph Talcott (November 16, 1669 - October 11, 1741) was the Governor of the Connecticut Colony from 1724 until his death in 1741.

Life and Death

Talcott was born in Hartford, Connecticut, the son of Lieutenant-Colonel John Talcott (1630-1688) and Helena Wakeman (1632-1674). He married Abigail Clark in 1693 and the couple had three sons. His second wife was Eunice Howell, with whom he had five more children.

Descended from one of Connecticut's founding settlers, Talcott was appointed an assistant (member of the governor's council) in 1711. He held several city and state offices; justice of the peace in 1705, and beginning in 1710, he was a Major in the First Regiment of the Colony of Connecticut. His position as Major continued to 1723. He was a member of the committee to lay out the town of Coventry in 1711. He owned property in several Connecticut towns. In May of 1714, he was appointed as a judge of the Hartford County Court, and he became Judge of the Superior Court of Hartford in May 1721.

In 1723, Talcott was elected Deputy Governor upon the death of Nathan Gold; then following the sudden death of Gurdon Saltonstall, he was the Governor. He was the first Connecticut Governor to be born in the state. He was reelected annually until his death, for a total of seventeen years and five months in office. This time was only surpassed by Gov. John Winthrop's eighteen years in office.

1. These are books written about some of my ancestors who were major people of the Mayflower and the founding of America. These books are:

2. Stephen Hopkins: The man who survived Jamestown and Saved Plymouth.

3. Pilgrims, The Native Americans, and The Colonies

4. Marooned: Jamestown, Shipwreck, and a New History of America's Origin

Stephen Hopkins, born 1582 and is the father of Oceanus who was born on the MAYFLOWER en route to America.

The Thanksgiving Story You've Probably Never Heard

Not everyone confessed the Pilgrim creed at the first gathering of what would become our national holiday. Maybe we don't have the pilgrims alone to thank for democracy.

Nov. 21, 2021

By Joseph Kelly

Mr. Kelly is the author of "Marooned: Jamestown, Shipwreck, and a New History of America's Origin."

The pilgrim William Bradford tells us about the first Thanksgiving. Winter was brutal. Snowbound in their hastily built houses, nearly every settler got sick; all were hungry, and half died. Spring followed, and with the help of Indians, the survivors reaped their first American harvest. English hunters went fowling in the woods, Massasoit brought in deer and about 90 Wampanoags, and everyone played games together and feasted for three days.

No matter when our families emigrated to America, we acknowledge these spiritual ancestors in a national rite every November, when we crowd around our dining room tables and feast on a traditional Thanksgiving meal of turkey and fixings.

As Nathaniel Philbrick put it in his best-selling "Mayflower," those odd, quaint fellows who had big-buckled shoes and hunted turkey with blunderbusses have come to "symbolize all that is good about America."

But the pilgrims (Bradford called them "saints") weren't the only settlers at the feast. Troublesome "strangers" who did not confess the Pilgrim creed were there, too.

One of the strangers was the historical figure you should be thinking about this Thanksgiving. You've probably never heard of Stephen Hopkins. He might change the way you think about the national holiday.

We don't know very much about him. Hopkins was born in 1581, about the same time Shakespeare married Anne Hathaway in Stratford. His family was neither poor nor rich. As a young man, Hopkins leased a farm, married, had children and lost his lease, and perhaps to mend his fortunes in 1609 he joined 500 other settlers headed for Jamestown, Virginia.

They sailed into a hurricane. Most of the ships staggered into Chesapeake Bay with shaken passengers and sea-sodden cargoes, but the flagship, the Sea Venture, never arrived. Its disappearance triggered the notorious "starving time" at Jamestown.

The Sea Venture didn't sink. Sailors and passengers bailed water for three days and nights until their tired bones could work no more. Just as they gave in to drowning, the ship ran aground on a shoal in the Mid-Atlantic. Across a lagoon, about a mile away, the cedars of Bermuda beckoned.

One hundred-fifty survivors found themselves marooned in a Garden of Eden. The uninhabited islands were full of pigs, fowl, fruit and fish. No turkey but plenty of pork to roast. Why not stay?

Reasoning things out, Stephen Hopkins stumbled upon the idea that made America. The Virginia Company failed to deliver the settlers to Jamestown, he argued, which released the settlers from their contract. The shipwreck dissolved it. The castaways were free to work for the company if they wanted, or they could choose to work for themselves.

Image

Jobson's cove in Bermuda. Credit...Tony Cenicola/The New York Times

On the deserted island, Hopkins came up with the social-contract theory of government about 40 years before Thomas Hobbes would write "Leviathan," almost 80 years before John Locke wrote his "Two Treatises of Government" and 166 years before Thomas Jefferson's Declaration of Independence.

In the wilderness of Bermuda, Hopkins persuaded most of the settlers to form a fledgling democracy.

But the company wouldn't have it. The governor insisted they were still under contract and must help build a ship that would carry them to Jamestown. He gave orders. The settlers dragged their feet. He threatened. They fled into the woods. Finally, the governor and his cronies turned Bermuda into a slave labor camp, and after nine months, under the threat of guns, the castaways were forced to embark for Virginia.

For his part in the "mutiny," Hopkins was sentenced to death, but he talked his way to clemency. He kept his head down. He served out his term of years, and then he returned to England. Shakespeare mocked and misrepresented his political theory in one of the last plays he ever wrote, "The Tempest," but otherwise Hopkins fell out of history. At least for 10 years.

Anchored off the coast of Massachusetts, William Bradford tells us, some "discontented" strangers started spreading a "mutinous" argument: Because the Mayflower had drifted so far off course, it was beyond the scope of the company's patent. "When they came ashore," the strangers insisted, they could "use their own liberty" to form a new government.

On Nov. 21, 1620, a remarkable document did just that. "We whose names are underwritten," it said, "covenant and combine ourselves into a civil body politic." We know this document today as the Mayflower Compact, a flagstone on the road to the United States Constitution. Forty-one men signed it, both saints and strangers.

Bradford said the "saints" wrote the compact to bring the "strangers" in line, and Philbrick claims that the compact was modeled on the "spiritual covenant" that had bound the pilgrims together in Holland. His later book, "Bunker Hill," treats the American Revolution as if it were the end of a pilgrims' progress. Boston in 1776 was the "shining city on a hill" prophesied by John Winthrop.

There's nothing radical about this version of history. Scholars have been telling us for the last hundred years that we can thank the pilgrims for democracy.

And yet, I've always thought it was a little odd that those secular ideals of natural rights so perfectly articulated by Thomas Jefferson started with people who outlawed dissent. Was freedom of religion really invented by people who hunted witches? Did our distinctly American notions of economic liberty come from people who scolded the poor for being discontent? Did democracy grow out of righteousness?

Probably not. It turns out that one of the Mayflower Compact's signers was a man named Stephen Hopkins. Most scholars today think he was the same Hopkins who was marooned on Bermuda, and that puts a new spin on the story. After all, the strangers' complaints about invalid company "patents" and settlers' liberty sound exactly like Hopkins's argument in Bermuda. And the Mayflower Compact itself establishes the same government of mutual consent that Hopkins nearly died trying to secure.

We've taken the Mayflower tale as gospel truth ever since it was rediscovered in the 1840s. But Hopkins's story suggests that we ought to take Bradford with a grain of salt. If we read with the slightest suspicion, we'll give credit where credit is due: More than likely, the Mayflower Compact was designed to protect the liberty of strangers from the tyranny of saints.

Maybe it's time to start thinking of ourselves as the descendants of strangers, the castaways of Jamestown and the unanointed of Plymouth Plantation. Starting this Thanksgiving, maybe we should eat barbecue.

Joseph Kelly, a professor of Irish and Irish American studies at the College of Charleston, is the author of "Marooned: Jamestown, Shipwreck, and a New History of America's Origin."

Follow The New York Times Opinion section on Facebook, Twitter (@NYTopinion) and Instagram.

My Norwegian Heritage

My biological dad was born in Moscow, Idaho. His mother, Mary Holten was born in 1879 in Hemnes, Akershus, Norway, to Ildri Johnsdatter (Fosseide), age 28, and Johan Olsen Holten, age 35.

This is what her bio looks like on Ancestry.com.
Mary Holten1879 • Hemne, South Trondelag, Norway
BIRTH1879 Hemne, South Trondelag, Norway
DEATH1969 Idaho, USA
sources (24)records (23)photos (3)

Family Info
Father	·	Johan Olsen Holten (1844–1904)
Mother	·	Ildri Johnsdatter (Fosseide) (1851–1888)
Spouse	·	Anton Andersen Saether (1884–1906)
Children	·	Irene (1905–2004)
Spouse	·	Henry Emil Erickson (1886–1978)
		Married 1907
Children	·	Irene Sather (1905–2004)
	·	Myrtle Bernice (1908–1989)
	·	John "Jobie" Emil (1909–2006)
	·	Myrtle B (1909–1988)
	·	Sally Eldora (Minnie) (1912–)
	·	Hazel Marguerite (1914–2000)
	·	Hazel Marguerite (1914–2002)
	·	Helen (1918–)
	·	Gladys Mae (1919–1976)
	·	Donald Dale (1922–2006)

Around 1902 Mary and her sister Karen, (who later married Newt Mickelbust) and their niece came to America by way of ship through Ellis Island. Which is why I wanted to go see Ellis Island for myself.

On December 22, 1904, Mary married Anton Andersen Saether, in Langdon, North Dakota. He died in 1906 in Royal, North Dakota, leaving her with small child, Irene. She traveled to Moscow, Idaho with her child to work as a camp cook for the threshing crew. It was there that she met Henry Emil Erickson, and they were married on November 25, 1907. She was 28 years old.

Her mother, Ildri, died in 1888 at the age of 37. He father Johan, died in 1904 at the age of 59. They had 4 children together.

Both of my grandparents, Mary Holten and Henry Emil Erickson generations go back to around 1544. That is 7 or maybe 8 great grandparents, on both sides.

I plan on taking a cruise up the fjords of the Norwegian coast in a few years with my daughter Kristal. This cruise that I want to take goes from Burgan on the coast of Norway all the way up to the very top of Norway and then back down. Stopping in about 15 port towns going up, dropping off supplies to these towns and then the same coming back down the coast. One of the towns that is a stopping point is the town of Trondheim. One of the coastal towns of my heritage.

To say that looking up ancestors is addictive is an understatement. I started out thinking that this would be as fun as sticking your finger down your throat and ended up being fascinated by all the different aspects of the research.

Mother and Dad

R ock Creek Grange, in the countryside of Potlach, Idaho is where Glen and Agnes Gilder met. He was 6'1", slender and very good looking. She was short, being all of 4'11", slender and very pretty. They both attended the Rock Creek Grange Hall dances. They meet, and then dance for a while and then Glen would get outside for a smoke and meet up with other guys at the dance, and they all would share in the mason jars of moonshine out back behind the grange. Then go back into the dance.

When I was in Jr. high, I remember I was getting ready for a dance, when mother and dad started telling me about how they met at those dances. At age 14, I just couldn't imagine that "old people" loved to dance, or as they put it, "cut a rug". They just laughed and said, "Oh yes, we did love to dance, and we were quite good at it too." Then I would see that faraway look in their eyes, as they were remembering when.

Later, when Glen was 26 and Agnes was 25, they both were afraid of her mother, Mary, so, after milking the dairy cows and chores were finished, they agreed to meet down the road, and together, in Glen's car, drove to Moscow, to the courthouse, had the Justice of the Peace marry them, and then they drove back to Agnes's mother's farm. Both Agnes and Glen did that night's milking of the Guernsey and Jersey cows. When the milking was finished, and everything was cleaned up, stalls "mucked out" and fresh hay put in the stalls, then they told her mother that they eloped. Her mother was so mad! Agnes was a fast milker and that meant that she was losing her best milker, well, only other milker besides herself. It didn't take long for Mary to get over being mad because Agnes came every morning and evening to do her usual share of the milking chores. They eloped; I had the big church wedding. Theirs lasted for well over 50 years while mine didn't last but 26 years.

In the 1990's Colin Raye sang a song that always reminded me of mother and dad. I 'll share it here. It's hard to believe that someone else had the same experience as mother and dad did, all those years ago.

Love, Me

I read a note my grandma wrote back in 1923
Grandpa kept it in his coat and he showed it once to me
He said, "Boy, you might not understand but a long, long time ago
Grandma's daddy didn't like me none but I loved your grandma so"

We had this crazy plan to meet and run away together
Get married in the first town we came to and live forever
But nailed to the tree where we were supposed to meet instead
I found this letter and this is what it said

If you get there before I do, don't give up on me
I'll meet you when my chores are through
I don't know how long I'll be but I'm not gonna let you down
Darling, wait and see

And between now and then 'til I see you again
I'll be loving you, love me

I read those words just hours before my grandma passed away
In the doorway of a church where me and grandpa stopped to pray
I know I'd never seen him cry in all my 15 years
But as he said these words to her, his eyes filled up with tears

If you get there before I do, don't give up on me
I'll meet you when my chores are through
I don't know how long I'll be but I'm not gonna let you down
Darling, wait and see

And between now and then 'til I see you again
I'll be loving you, love me.

Goals and Adventures

I n a few days, I will be having a total knee replacement at a hospital and then a short stay in a nursing home that has a great physical therapy (P.T.) department. My girls sat me down and had a "tough love" and "heart to heart talk" with me that they are not medical people and that it's not fair to expect my friends to take care of me 24/7. And that I need to go to a nursing home to have the nursing take care of me and the Physical Therapy dept. made me do the exercises. Now I understand what older persons feel when they are told that they are going to a nursing home. Noooo..

I had that "deer in the headlights" look and emotions of what they were telling me, but it didn't take me long to come to the realization that they were right. There is a saying that how you exercise the replaced knees or hips in the first 3 to 4 weeks is all the movement you will ever get from that replacement for the rest of your life. I know myself well enough by now to know that I will be a wimp and lazy when it comes to exercising the knee and all my muscles. So, I became proactive about my care, and I called the nursing home with the best P.T. department and let them know that I wanted a room with them.

I still have a lot of adventures that I want to go on. The first of which is either later this year or next year, to fly back to Pennsylvania and with my cousin Susan walk the Civil War Battle fields, go to Philadelphia, and hopefully be there when Kristal is there working and tour with both the sights, and historical values of that great city. To go back to Vermont and visit sights that my newly found cousins wanted to show me, the first time we came to their great state. I want to travel to Yellowstone Park, yes, I live so close to the park, but have never been. I have dreams of going to The Grand Canyon and to learn how to weave rugs like the Navajo women do. I still have plans to see Norway. I can't do any of these things with the current condition of my knee(s), so, first, the knee surgery, then the P.T. rehab and the long haul of exercising and walking distances and then the adventures.

Making it through the Storm

Yes, I have made it through the storms that have happened in my life. But somehow with age and the grace of God, I have become more contented with myself. Along with that contentment comes the ability to not take any "guff" on harm that someone might want to inflict upon me. I will dish it right back at that person. I am a much more contended woman and somehow feel wiser. Maybe because of the storms that have happened in my life. I know that life has high peaks and deep valleys, and I know it is how we handle these highs and lows that make for a life. I believe that God will have his arm around me during the lows and happy for me with the high mountain peaks of my life. I also know that God's arms will be stretched wide for me at the very end of my life.

AUTHOR'S PHOTO GALLERY
OVER THE YEARS

This is my recent photo

This is me, the very first day that I came to live permanently
with "Mother" and "Dad", my mom's parents. Notice the
wagon wheel gate that is right above my head. This is the gate
that I would swing on while waiting for my biological dad.
A dad who never came, but just a few times.

My first-grade picture, the age of when I first would
be waiting for my biological parents.

My Senior Picture

"Mother" and myself

"Dad" Walking me down the Aisle

Mother and Dad's 50th wedding anniversary. This is how
they looked all during my Jr. high and high school years.
This was taken when my oldest child was 1 year old.

This a mystical picture of the log house that I grew up

This quilt is made with Civil War Reproduction fabrics

Fall Foliage in Montgomery, Vermont

Amish made Wedding Ring Quilt.

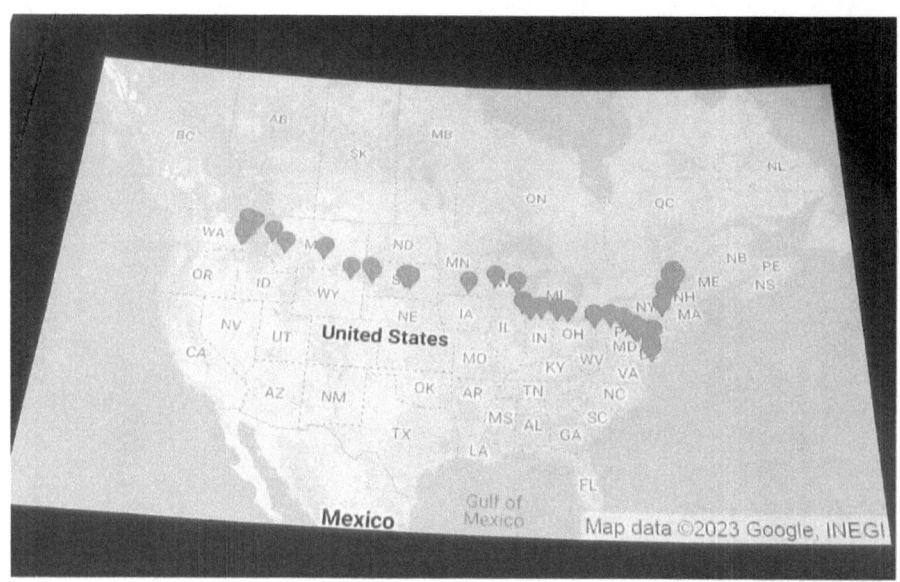

This is the google map of my route to
Pennsylvania and Vermont